BEYOND THE
BLUE MOUNTAIN

BEYOND THE BLUE MOUNTAIN

ALEC MCDONALD

Matador
9 Priory Business Park,
Wistow Road, Kibworth Beauchamp,
Leicestershire. LE8 0RX
Tel: 0116 279 2299
Email: books@troubador.co.uk
Web: www.troubador.co.uk/matador
Twitter: @matadorbooks

ISBN 978 1800462 090

British Library Cataloguing in Publication Data.
A catalogue record for this book is available from the British Library.

Printed and bound by CPI Group (UK) Ltd, Croydon, CR0 4YY
Typeset in 12pt Adobe Garamond Pro by Troubador Publishing Ltd, Leicester, UK

Matador is an imprint of Troubador Publishing Ltd

To my children, their children, and their children.

We are the Pilgrims, master; we shall go
Always a little further; it may be
Beyond that last blue mountain barred with snow
Across that angry or that glimmering sea.

James Elroy Flecker

Foreword

This book began life as a memoir for the extended family who for years have pressed me to write down the story of my life. It was initially not intended for publication. My intention was to paint a picture of the life and times of the family of an intelligence officer. However, as the work progressed, I changed my mind about publication, persuaded that it would be of interest to a wider readership while persuading myself that I could allow myself some latitude in writing about my career when there is so much information about intelligence procedures and organisation in the public domain. I thus changed course taking greater care in writing about my work.

In its form the book is episodic and picaresque in character with the protagonist confronting one challenge after another, scarcely believing the turn of events. While it contains much about my work as an intelligence officer, there is a great deal more left unsaid and there are no sensational disclosures. Such glimpses as I give of operations are of long ago and nothing I write threatens national security. The few names I mention are well known and dead, while others I describe might be recognised by my contemporaries.

I have not sought permission to publish as I know it would be refused on principle. The book and its author will be frowned on by the Service and by many, perhaps most, colleagues but I hope nevertheless that they will enjoy the ride and those of my generation hear again the trumpet call.

I have written from memory supported by old passports, YHA cards and other flotsam and jetsam. My children provided a further memory bank and I thank them and in particular my daughter Catherine who kept a professional eye on the work in progress and has masterminded publication. I also thank Eve Leeds, the daughter of my companion in Spitsbergen, for photographs and information about her father. Finally, I express my admiration of Myst Ltd for the enhancement of damaged photographs and the appended map.

Early years

I am Ronald Alexander McDonald, Ronald after my father and Alexander after the cooing of a nurse in the hospital where I was born on the 1st of September 1930. The nurse, a Scots lassie, called me 'the wee Sandy' which seems to have stirred my father's Scottish roots: he vetoed Valentine, the name my mother had in mind. Whatever its initial colour, my hair was always black and I have always been known simply as Alec.

Grandpa McDonald had taken the road south from Glasgow and found work in the Liverpool docks, rising to warehouse supervisor. My father was the youngest of the ten surviving children: Edgar, Jessie, Clara, Flora, Allan, Ethel, Elsie, Roy, Rona, Ronald. They seem to have lived in some comfort in Bootle in a house known ironically in the family as College View, after the proliferation of surrounding streets with college names. Grandpa McDonald died in his late fifties before I was born and I only know Grandma McDonald from a family snapshot in which she is wearing a large cloche hat and a grim expression.

My mother, born in 1897, was one of the ten children born to the Spencer family, eight of whom survived: Henry, Harold, Annie, Alice, Agnes (my mother), Theresa, Lucy and May. The family moved

1

from St Helens to Liverpool in the early 1900s and settled in Old Swan, a poor district with a large Irish community, among whom as Catholics they fitted in well though regarding themselves superior as homegrown Lancashire Catholics. The family was not poor and would indignantly reject any such suggestion, but there was little to spare and little space. My mother recalled that when she was growing up only her parents sat at meals while the rest of the family stood round the table. She left school at thirteen and when old enough was taken on by J. Lyons & Co., a nationwide catering company with its ubiquitous high street tea shops.

At work she met my father, a fellow clerk, who had eventually found work at Lyons after being unemployed in the depression that followed the First World War. His war service was inglorious. Called up on turning eighteen he was sent after training to the front, where he was in one sense fortunate to catch trench fever and for this or some other reason was not called upon to perform heroics, unlike his older brother Allan, who was killed in Flanders.

As a condition for marriage to Agnes my father had to convert to Catholicism. This is a laborious and intensive process, as it is intended to be, and a convert bears the added weight of high expectation. I noticed in later years that my father was far more observant than my mother who missed Mass most Sundays, persuading herself that intention to attend met her obligation. They married in 1929, both were in their early thirties, and for their honeymoon made a day trip to St Malo in Brittany, the only occasion that either of them ventured abroad.

They set up house at 23 Woodchurch Road next door to the Spencers at No 25, the effect of which was to immerse my father in Catholic life. Grandma Spencer, a frail and seemingly unassertive woman, had an aura of sanctity about her and was revered by her daughters over whom she ruled without lifting a finger. The elderly parents were looked after by Auntie May, the stay-at-home daughter, who took in sewing for a living. She had her mother's saint-like aura and was active in church affairs and led pilgrimages to Lourdes.

There was no sign of religious fervour in Grandpa Spencer. Whatever he thought he kept his head down and watched the passing day in silence from his rocking chair. His only interest appeared to be tomatoes. Charged one day to look after 'the boys', my younger brother and me, he took us with him on the weekly visit to his greenhouse to harvest the crop which was later sold illegally at the back door. The greenhouse was in Morton at the far end of the Wirral peninsular and it took a three-stage journey to get there, first the tram to Pier Head, then ferry and bus. None of us could think of what to say to the other until, on passing the signpost for Bidston, Grandpa Spencer said, 'There is a mill on Bidston Hill and if it's not gone it's there still'. This stayed with him throughout the day and he recited it whenever the silence became oppressive, including back at home as we sat in silence listening to the creak of his chair and the slow tick tock of the kitchen clock. In appearance he was not unlike W C Fields with a large pock-marked nose.

In later years, having moved away, we used to go back to Liverpool for our summer holidays, my father coming for a week or two. We always stayed with Auntie Alice. She had the space and was better provided for than her siblings as her husband was 'on the monthly', having risen above weekly wages. Uncle Arthur was a qualified electrician employed by the North West Electricity Board in the Liverpool transformer station. His speech was slow and measured and unexcitable. He cycled to work and on return home would remove his shoes to reveal saturated socks and a glimpse of his long johns. What we were waiting for was the Daily Mirror, which he took, folded in eight, from his pocket. Our only interest was the daily cartoon of Jane, a young woman unable to dress without interruption and whose skirt was repeatedly pulled down by the irrepressible Fritzie, her dachshund. We were four boys engaged in this furtive activity: my brother and I, Alice's son, and Theresa's son, who was living with the family following his mother's death from pernicious anaemia, as leukaemia was then commonly known.

All three of Theresa's children were abandoned by their father and thrown on the mercies of the family. The eldest, Marjorie, went to live at No 25, an unenviable fate for a teenage girl. Phillip went to Alice and the baby, unusually named Helene, was adopted by Auntie Annie and Uncle Bill who had no children, not I am sure for want of trying. Though nothing was ever said, there was a sense that Annie had not done well for herself by marrying a man whose job was to clean the lights in the Mersey Tunnel. Uncle Bill was the archetypal Irish scouser: small, dapper, endlessly cheerful, quick on the repartee, he would break into a little tap dance when invention flagged. He saucily commended his daughter to our attention; 'ooh, she's a lovely judy'.

For us boys, Annie and Billy were fun and we enjoyed their lack of decorum, all the more because of the family reservations of which we were supposed not to be aware. Auntie Annie would rattle her false teeth and pull faces. She told lavatory humour jokes which my mother also enjoyed despite her feeble protests, 'oh, give over, Annie'. In the game 'I went on my holiday and packed…' Annie's first item was always a pair of knickers followed by other indecorous items on succeeding turns. There were the tongue twisters we were made to repeat until we stumbled: chew chew chew till your jaws drop.

While the Spencer family was cohesive and close at hand, Father's siblings were scattered over north Liverpool requiring multiple tram rides to reach them. Moreover, as no one had telephones, all the visits were made on spec and our welcome, one of hastily concealed dismay. The menfolk returning from work were astounded to find four McDonalds eating their supper. Uncle Jack, a carpenter, said, 'Oh, hello Ronald' then spent the rest of our visit supposedly sharpening his tools in the cellar. It was much the same with Uncle Edgar, the eldest of the family, a bachelor lodging with one of the sisters, except that he went back out after a few minutes on his way, we were told, to play billiards at the working men's club.

For us boys these visits were an ordeal. Dragged halfway across Liverpool, we were put on display and endured hours of boredom with only curiosity to sustain us. The unexpected occasionally happened. At Auntie Clara's, I had an entrancing first game of Monopoly and at

Uncle Henry's we were subjected to electric shocks from a scientific toy or therapy device. We sat round in a circle, hands joined, while Henry manipulated the voltage so that at times we all shook uncontrollably. The driving force behind the visits was my mother, her mania reaching its ultimate expression in the visit to 'little Annie', a school friend, who lived in Amlwch on the north coast of Anglesey, a train ride of several hours from Liverpool. As usual, no arrangements had been made and by great good fortune 'little Annie' was at home to receive our ten-minute visit, which was all there was time for before setting off on the return journey.

As an infant I gave my parents a lot of worry. In those pre-immunisation days children were exposed to a frightening array of illnesses: diphtheria, tuberculosis, polio, measles, scarlet fever, mumps. At the age of three I contracted measles with adverse effects. Abscesses developed in both ears and, in the right ear, the infection spread to the mastoid bone requiring surgery, with the result that I finished up with no hearing in that ear and impaired hearing in the left. I also caught scarlet fever and spent weeks in an isolation hospital. For good measure, I had my tonsils and adenoids removed and can only think that this was done to improve my chances if I fell victim to diphtheria and the risk of suffocation.

When I was five, I started school at St Oswald's RC Primary School and was taught by the nuns from the convent adjacent to the church. I was frightened of the nuns with their strange clothing and, when pulled affectionately to them, struggled to break free from their voluminous skirts. In my mind's eye, I see my classroom with benches and slates and ABC books of an earlier age. I was already reading and had no difficulty with text, but some of the associated pictures were hard to make out. G for example showed a girl in Victorian dress sitting in a carriage and, below, the strange words 'Nan sits in the gig'. J is for Jasper was illustrated by a drawing of an irregular shape blotched here and there by shading. What on earth was it? After much thought, I concluded that a 'jasper' was a soiled tea-towel.

At Christmas, my father took me to the children's party given by Lyons. It was a lavish affair with lots to eat and games in which I took part tentatively, rather overwhelmed by the numbers of children. We sat down to watch a stage performance. A man came down from the stage to select a boy and a girl and, to my horror, picked me out. I was dragged on to the stage and there, beside a simpering girl, I was called upon to sing 'Animal Crackers in my Soup'. I willed the ground to open and swallow me up. The music started and we had, if not to sing along with Shirley Temple, at least to mime the words and actions. In contrast to the girl who threw herself around, I stood rooted to the spot, mute and scowling, my head bowed, staring at my shoes. I held on. At last the music stopped and I could escape and return to anonymity. What an ordeal, as great as any I have endured.

My school days at St Oswald's were cut short by the momentous decision of my parents to quit the Spencer nest of Woodchurch Road. Whether this was to break free of the Spencer grip or was due to my mother's aspirational urge or simply to escape the contagions of Liverpool, we moved to Eastham, a village to the south of Birkenhead on the other side of the Mersey. Eastham was known as the Richmond-on-Thames of Merseyside, as I am sure my mother knew in choosing our destination, but I expect the decision derived from an accumulation of factors, including perhaps the promotion of my father at work.

There were signs of this in our new life. New furniture arrived including the must-have of the day, a radiogram in the form of a chest, the lid of which opened to reveal gramophone and radio promising access to dozens of stations in an illuminated array of different colours. All these acquisitions were surely bought on the 'never-never', as must also have been Arthur Mee's Children's Encyclopaedia bought from a door-to-door salesman. We had the complete set of ten volumes. Nowadays condemned because of incorrect attitudes, for example, 'the Kaffirs live happily in kraals', the encyclopaedia was nevertheless a window on the world and we pored over the pictures if not the text.

The most striking change in our lives was the cornucopia of cakes that graced our table. My father had become the cashier for the roundsmen delivering Lyons' products, taking in their cash at the end of the day. On Saturdays they also turned in perishable goods which were then shared out. My father, now cycling to work, raced home with his saddlebag bulging with cakes and melting ice-cream. We waited for him, spoon in hand, ready to scoop it onto the plate: a brick of vanilla, a slab of pink, white and green. What cakes had he brought? Chocolate Gateau, Walnut Cake with cream filling, Victoria Sandwich, Battenberg, Chocolate Log, Madeira Cake and the humble Swiss Roll which we steadily ate our way through during the week to clear the decks for Saturday.

Before many months had passed we were on the move again, this time to Brighton where our stay was short, Father perhaps filling a holiday vacancy, before moving on to his eventual destination, Cadby Hall, Lyons' headquarters in south-east London. The schools were on holiday and my brother and I spent a lot of the time indoors with chicken pox. We left Brighton to stay at the home of a work colleague in London before settling for a longer stay at rented accommodation in Lee Green near Lewisham. We had the lower floor of a detached house in whose upper storey lived a Charlton Athletic footballer, rumoured to be paid the then princely wage of £10 a week.

I went to St Winifred's, a nearby Catholic school. I was a quiet introspective boy, very shy, but well used to starting at strange schools. I was not afraid of them. I had learned that I could get by doing nothing and avoiding attracting attention, like a mouse silently watching and judging when it was safe to move. It went well except for the day the teacher called me to face the class beside a girl also with a Scottish name. She draped her arms round us and presented us to the class as descendants of ferocious clan chiefs. I kept my eyes down. It was my worst moment since the Lyons party.

We were not to stay long with the footballer. The next move would be final: my parents were about to buy a house, the culmination of their aspirational quest. My father evidently could now afford a mortgage and they had enough for the deposit on the £650 house. One day we went with Mother to Bexleyheath to sign on the dotted line in a temporary office on the land on which the housing estate was being built. The houses were all semi-detached in two designs. Asked to choose by Mother, we chose the one with the mock gable; we also chose the colours of the complimentary lampshades. The choice of blue for one bedroom was a ghastly mistake.

During 1938 we moved in and began a settled life, my mother at last in her own home. We were old enough to go out to play on our own in the tranquil estate and on tricycles and skates we raced round the looped streets. I joined the library and devoured books so rapidly that the librarian restricted me to one book a day. Defiant, I took out Oliver Twist and regretted it but, determined not to admit defeat, I ground my way through its 800 pages. We played the records accumulated by my parents in their salad days over and over on the radiogram. We cut out from the Sunday People newspaper the coupons to join the Cheery Coons, a promotion inconceivable today, based on a strip cartoon in the paper in which Ebb and Flo, black, got up to their tricks. We only had enough coupons to be entry-level Coons, but the yellow and gold badges with the heads of Ebb and Flo were very satisfying and we wore them proudly to church.

My brother and I went to Bedonwell Hill Primary School, a ten-minute walk away. In contrast to the dark old church schools I was familiar with, it was bright and open, purpose-built by the local authority. I adopted a low profile as usual and parried the attempts of the girl in the adjacent desk to be friendly. A girl! Girls had never crossed our path apart from Helene and we had managed to avoid having anything to do with her. I was embarrassed by having to sit next to a girl and I decided not to tell anyone at home about it.

A surprise event, to us boys anyway, was the birth of a brother in February 1939. Hailed by the pious as a Gift from God, it brought Grandma Spencer to Bexleyheath to see the child. The gift, alas, came with chronic asthma and he struggled to breathe throughout his life, dying of heart failure aged thirty-two.

World War II

The family idyll was doomed to be of short duration. In the month following the birth of our new brother, Czecho-Slovakia was invaded and Chamberlain warned that an attack on Poland would lead to war. The ensuing months had no effect on our schoolboy life and it was only after the declaration of war that things started happening with the issue of gas masks in square cardboard boxes, ration books and identity cards. In the back garden a large hole was dug in which to bury our Anderson shelter, a corrugated iron box six and a half feet long and four and a half feet wide. How small it was.

In anticipation of bombing, evacuation of children and mothers with child from major centres of population got underway. Evacuation was voluntary but my parents embraced it, expecting that the not too distant docks and the Woolwich Arsenal would be targets. We were, thus, swept up in the first wave. Surprisingly, we were sent the short distance to Rough Common, a village near Canterbury, and lodged in a sparsely furnished Army hiring of which the young wife of an Army officer was the sole occupant. She was rather brisk and Mother did not take to her and it was as well that we moved within days to a conventional house with chickens in the back garden. The weeks passed and, in the absence of the expected air-raids, we joined the drift back to London. This was the period of the Phoney War as it came to be called.

In the summer of 1940, after the fall of France, a second wave of evacuation started in anticipation of the coming blitz. My parents held true to their faith in evacuation. It was a fateful decision that would undo all they had achieved. The house was to sustain some damage from a landmine which fell nearby but it was minor and they could have taken their chances. However, the family split up. My brother and I were evacuated to an unknown destination, Mother and the baby went to North Wales to live with Jessie, my father's eldest sister, while Father stayed on and slept at work as a member of the Fire Watch team. Showing no apparent emotion, Mother handed us over at the designated railway station with, as specified, a luggage label with name attached to the lapel, a packed lunch and our by now inseparable companion, the gas mask. We caught a glimpse of her waving as we boarded the train but for our part we were excited. The journey seemed interminable, with long halts at stations from which the names had been removed to baffle invading Germans.

We eventually arrived without knowing it at South Molton in North Devon. A bus took us to a hall where we were seated in rows under the scrutiny of the good ladies of the town lining the walls. At a signal they pounced, intent on bagging the cleanest. A tall portly lady in a hat claimed us and bore us away to 37 South Street, which was to be our home for the next year. It was by then dusk. We supped on gooseberry pie in the kitchen in the gathering gloom. A small gnome-like man came in with a branding-iron in his hand and made great play of branding the family dog. This was Mr Courtney, blacksmith, pater familias of three children: the eldest, a daughter who was married and had left home, a son approaching call-up age who was an apprentice carpenter and a second younger daughter who worked in a shop. The Courtneys put themselves out for us: the son shared with his father; the daughter moved in with her mother freeing her bedroom for us. We could not have landed better.

The evacuees, seemingly all boys, were not assimilated with local schoolchildren. Our makeshift school was set up in a church hall with the older ones facing one way and the younger ones the other, thirty or forty all told. There was a teacher at each end and a third who patrolled the classroom keeping order. All three had canes and retribution was swift, across the palm: no talking, let alone larking about. My low-profile posture was well suited to that environment and though I did not escape the cane the atmosphere was benign. Of the schoolwork, I remember little apart from grappling with difficult fractions, which stood me in good stead for the Eleven Plus examination. In the weeks before the exam, I was coached after school with a classmate from Bexleyheath by his mother, a teacher, who had joined her son in South Molton. I took the examination and some weeks later the headmaster burst into the classroom with a piece of paper which he thrust under my nose. It was a letter from the Education Department of Kent County Council in which I saw that I was third or fourth on the list of those awarded a special place.

In our year in South Molton we saw and learned much. We watched Mr Courtney at work in his smithy. Although he worked during the week at an agricultural repair shop, he continued to shoe a horse from time to time and, on one exciting occasion, he made and fitted the metal rim of a cartwheel. As the hot rim was hammered into place, the wheel burst into flames then creaked as the rim tightened its grip when the flames were doused. The long garden of the house met at right angles the adjoining garden of a farrier and corn merchant, also a Courtney. Now and then we took his carthorse to its field at the end of the day, or rather the horse took us, our sole contribution being to open and close the gate. We went on outings to Exmoor with the ladies of the Mothers' Union to pick whortleberries. We were taken to the seaside near Barnstable. The Courtneys' son would come back from work with wild birds' eggs in his lunch box and I assembled quite a collection, which I still have among effects in storage in a box unopened for decades. I collected cap badges, buttons and other military insignia. South Molton was not insulated from the war. There were soldiers around from a nearby unit and the town was an R and R resort. You occasionally saw disfigured men with shiny-pink skin grafts or a couple of Sergeant Majors striding along in undress uniform, taking their exercise.

We did not miss our parents. It was not as if we had lost them; they were just off-stage, waiting in the wings. For all the kindly ministrations of the Courtneys, we felt a sense of independence, that we were on our own. I was a reserved and rather intense boy, always busy in my own world. I did not seek friends and had none except for my brother. We gained much from our stay in South Molton, a boyhood paradise, in self-confidence and in the breadth of experience it provided. In mid-August 1941, our parents were ready to take us back. We said goodbye, boarded the Greyhound bus and left with hardly a backward look, intent on what lay ahead.

Mother's first step in bringing the family back together was to get my father out of London. Accordingly, he threw over his seventeen-year career with Lyons and moved to a clerical job with Vauxhall Motors in Luton, ironically a potential target of attack as manufacturer of Bedford trucks for the Army. Mother and baby came down from Wales and we came back by the long and complex bus journey from Devon. As displaced persons from London we came under the care of the council. Our new home consisted of two rooms, a living room and bedroom in which all five of us slept, and use of the kitchen and bathroom. Our landlady was a young woman called Phyllis whose husband was away in the RAF. My mother in due course learnt from her that her husband had been a trombone player in a dance band before call-up. She was very forbearing and we kept out of each other's way.

The address was 197 Cutenhoe Road, mercifully at the convenient end of that long road which branches off the London road and at the time formed the southern boundary of Luton with fields beyond. It also afforded the most direct route to Vauxhall Motors for the Panzer Division. As a counter-measure, giant paraffin stoves were set at intervals on both sides of the road which when lit would give out clouds of black smoke to confuse the enemy. Also lining the road were mustard gas detectors. These were square boards set on the top of poles coated with a substance that changed colour when droplets of the gas fell on it. At home, we had to have black-out curtains over the windows at night for fear that the merest chink of light would bring down death and destruction. We felt we were now really in the war zone.

Needless to say, all this was subsumed in the daily realities of life, such as going to the Co-op for our rations. First the ration books were checked and the various entitlements worked out. The counter assistant then cut from the slabs of butter and cheese on the counter an estimation of the amount required, which was then weighed and adjusted as necessary. Two ounces per person of butter and cheese a week; in the butchers' 1 shilling and tuppence worth of meat and so on. Service was slow; you joined the queue and waited your turn. Queueing was part of your war effort.

The start of the new school year approached and we went to the school outfitters to get my uniform. Luton Modern School, soon to be restyled Grammar School, had agreed to take me and, trying on the blazer and cap, I saw myself for the first time in traditional schoolboy garb. The school colours, unloved and known as rhubarb and custard, were a muted red and yellow and the school crest showed three swags of wheat and the motto 'Ubi Semen Ibi Messis' – 'where the seed, there the harvest'. I was excited and apprehensive. I was aged ten, about to turn eleven.

School

At the school door, the new boys were drawn aside and checked in. I was directed to go and wait outside classroom No 1 where I stood, bewildered, as boys of all sizes streamed past along the corridor, wondering if I had heard correctly. A teacher, gown flapping, powered past. His voice boomed out: 'Put tha bum t'anchor, Goliath'. It belonged, as I learned later, to Mr Woodcock whose nickname in a boys' school can be left to the imagination. I was to find that I was the smallest boy in the school, measured by the school nurse at 4 feet 2¾ inches.

I was joined outside classroom No 1 by others not attending the Church of England morning prayers. In due course, we were summoned and ushered into the back of the assembly hall to hear words of welcome from the Headmaster and the allocation of classes read out by the Second Master. I strained to hear my name as he rattled through form after form and just caught my name among those destined for 1c.

The form master, Mr Partridge, was a grim-looking man with steel-rimmed glasses who appeared sightless when he took them off to clean them. He took us for French. Instead of launching straight into 'je suis tu es' we practiced the twelve vowel sounds of French which he demonstrated with facial contortions. This went on for weeks before we were given conventional textbooks and entered the world of Monsieur Dupont and family.

I sat out of name order at the front of the class because of my deafness and adopted my habitual head-down posture. To my surprise and embarrassment, I came top of the class in the end-of-term examinations and in second place the following term, despite higher marks, overtaken by an evacuee, two years older, who had been put in the class. At the beginning of the summer term we were both promoted to 1a. Catching up was a challenge but in the following year in 3a (the A stream omitted the second year) I gradually got on terms with the class leaders and found that I could compete. At last, after all those timid school years, I came out of my shell.

There were a lot of evacuees in the school or more accurately 'displaced persons' from families who had moved out of London to escape the bombing, as indeed we had. The school designed for 400 pupils was bursting at the seams with over 600, which included part of another school functioning independently. The largest contingent among those not attending morning prayers were the boys from Jewish families who spilled over into two classrooms for their own prayers. We Catholics were few, perhaps half a dozen, and we spent the time swinging our heels. Over the years, I formed a close friendship with a kindred spirit and we amused ourselves by composing imaginary letters to the Pope seeking guidance, for instance, about the doctrinal orthodoxy of Mr Parry, the R.I. teacher, who had declared that Mary Magdalene was probably a prostitute.

Luton Council found us a council house on the other side of Luton in Leagrave, an invisible sort of place at the end of a ribbon development consisting of a string of houses, a pub, a council estate and, somewhere in the hinterland, the Electrolux factory. Our house was one of a terrace with tunnels through to the back gardens; at one end our road petered out in a field. Mother put a good face on it but the irony of our new status cannot have escaped her: the upward trajectory of her life had taken a downward turn to a point below which she had started. My father knocked together a ramshackle henhouse for half a dozen bedraggled chickens who at times produced more eggs than we could deal with. Nourished by their other product, the rhubarb stood shoulder high, its stalks as thick as a man's wrist and inedible.

The house was a good twenty minutes' walk from the bus stop and buses were infrequent with no meaningful timetable. You simply waited until a bus arrived and hoped it would not be full. Father cycled to work, Mother walked to her job in the Electrolux factory and, until we got our bikes, we had a two-bus journey to school. Once we had the bikes there was no excuse not to attend church, also inconveniently located. Mother saw to it that her husband and sons fulfilled their duties though she herself, dressed in her Sunday best, did not get beyond the garden gate on Sunday mornings, persuading herself as usual that her intention to go to Mass met her obligation. My brother and I attended Sunday School and I went so far as to join the choir. I had a nice treble voice but found it difficult to sing in tune which seemed not to matter much in the tuneless chanting we did.

Despite appearances I was not a religious boy. I lacked faith and was uncomfortable about priests. As a child I had seen how these supernatural beings, on visits to the house, reduced it to whispers out of veneration of their powers. During church services, when all around bowed the head, I watched the priest like a hawk in the hope of seeing these powers in action. However, I kept my doubts to myself and limited myself to asking awkward questions at Sunday school. I even had a short career as an altar boy in the hope of getting my hands on the incense burner. I had my chance one Sunday at Benediction after Sunday school. Swinging the censer billowing forth clouds of smoke in ever increasing arcs, I turned to grin at my friends in the pews and caught the censer on the corner of the altar rail, discharging its contents.

At the beginning of the third year at school the class advanced to

4a. Noisy and active, we were kept in hand by discipline but some teachers responded to our ebullience, notably the English teacher who took great interest in the little magazine we created. Under the title 'Journal de Liberté' it contained articles written by three or four of us and was printed by the father of a classmate who ran a printing business. Unfortunately, the type setter made a mistake and the title came out as 'Journal de Jiberté'. Nonetheless, we were very pleased with it and invited contributions for a second edition. Dissension ensued. One contribution read:

> The boy stood on the burning deck
> His pocket full of crackers
> One went down his trouser leg
> And blew off both his knackers

The editorial committee felt that it lowered the tone but the aspiring poet, a confident and shameless country boy, insisted that it was exactly what the 'Journal de Jiberté' did need. We gave up, perhaps realising that we had little more to say.

Though I slipped down a few places in class ranking, I finished the year in better shape than my subject reports suggested I deserved: talkative, untidy, easily distracted, impetuous, careless, lacks concentration, below his best, could do better, must do better and so on. The year of reckoning lay ahead, School Certificate year, and my first term in 5a was a disaster. I came bottom of the class. The teachers were aghast and the Headmaster wrote that I might have to be held back a year. I even came bottom in a subject in which I thought I had made a particular effort. I was horrified and ashamed.

What had happened? My fall was due to a mix of over-confidence, distraction, and the absence of Mother. The first was self-evident and the last was due to the approaching end of Grandma Spencer. The daughters were summoned to her bedside and Mother was away for more than two months as the saintly old lady, despite her yearning for eternal life, hung grimly on to the one she had.

The distraction was the relationship I formed with a boy of my own age in a lower class at school who lived across the road. I was well aware of his existence but had not tried to get to know him or he me but, encountering him one day, I found that beneath his quiet diffident manner lay an irreverent sense of humour. We would meet up after school and roam the fields or loiter with local friends of his. As I got to know him better, I found that he had no particular interests, little regard for school, no apparent aims or ambitions, no strong views. He seemed adrift in life but comfortable with it. From the little he said about his home life, I understood that his father had walked out and that his mother let him do what he liked. His insouciance may not therefore have been all it seemed but it was infectious.

Unchecked in my mother's absence, I let schoolwork slide. Not totally though: I had developed an obsession with chemistry. In the school laboratory we had watched and participated in the analysis of metal salts. I was captivated by the dazzling yellow precipitate in one test, the purple vapour of iodine in another and by antimony bursting into red flames in chlorine. I wanted to do these things myself. I bought a heavy book entitled Inorganic Chemistry and set about creating a home laboratory.

I needed to be stopped there and then but, unrestrained, I found in Bedford a shop that sold test tubes, flasks and the like and in Luton a chemist prepared to sell me the various chemicals I wanted including, to my surprise, hydrochloric and sulphuric acid. I set up my laboratory in the sloping cupboard under the stairs and repeated some of the tests we had done at school. After school one afternoon with both parents at work, I decided to show my brother how to make chlorine. It was simple enough and I was soon filling large bottling jars with the green gas. When the jars were full, the gas rolled down the sides and started to fill the bath in which I was conducting the experiment. We fled downstairs, opening the front and back doors, and ran into the garden hoping the gas would disperse before Father got home.

Undeterred by this reckless venture, I pressed on with my ambition to make a firework. I packed my home-made gunpowder in the outer casing of a torch battery and set it alight in the garden. It lacked the sparkle of a firework and burned with an intense purplish flame like a blow-torch. I judged it safe to be to be lit inside the house and at Christmas unveiled my indoor firework improved by the addition of iron filings which I hoped would give it some sparks. I stood it on the tiled surface surround of the hearth and we stood back to watch it with the light turned off. The room quickly filled with choking smoke and we all ran out to the garden, coatless into the cold night. The residue cooled to form a black glass-like knob fused with the ceramic of the tile and irremovable. Mother was not pleased.

After the Christmas break, I returned to school subdued but defiant. I got down to work and, by the end of term, had regained most of the lost ground and went on to do well enough in the School Certificate examination to proceed to the Sixth Form. My parents were inordinately proud of me. In their eyes the School Certificate conferred status. They envisaged framing and hanging it in the hall as they had seen in a neighbour's house and Father said that it would qualify me for an apprenticeship at Vauxhall Motors. No, no, I said, I would be staying on at school and go on to university. They were impressed and not a little sceptical. We were not of the university-going social class, was it not aiming too high? Very few school-leavers, less than three per cent, went to university. I too harboured doubts: would I be up to it? How would I get there, and to Cambridge in particular? In my imaginings, it always had to be Cambridge from that day in the playground at St Winifred's when, faced by boys demanding to know which side I supported in the Boat Race, I replied Cambridge to my cost.

September 1945. Now in the Lower Sixth, life was very gentlemanly and relaxed. French, Latin, Spanish and German were my subjects, the last two new. I greatly enjoyed learning the languages but dropped German at the end of the year and switched to Art for my fourth subject, for me an easy option. I put my energies into Spanish, enjoying the literature as well as the language. One of our set books was an episode taken from a 16th century picaresque novel in which the protagonist, a rascally boy, Lazarillo, moves from master to master, in our episode a blind beggar. Answering the question about the book in the end of term examination, one of the class wrote the 'e' in beggar so that it appeared to be a 'u'. This gave rise to much hilarity in the class and probably also in the staff common room but our teacher affected not to notice, presumably judging it to be the best of his options.

Outside school, there were developments in my scouting career in which I had risen to Patrol Leader and, having passed the myriad tests required for First Class, my uniform was festooned with badges and stripes. One evening, the troop was visited by the organiser of the touring Ralph Reader Gang Show foraging for talent for the forthcoming performance in Luton. The show consisted of songs and sketches performed by local scouts led by a young professional in scout uniform. I was roped in and, after learning the song-book and one rehearsal, I appeared on the stage of the Grand Theatre, Luton, for two performances, belting out 'I'm riding along on the crest of the wave' in the chorus. I also performed in a two-boy sketch as a snooty toff sitting next to a social inferior at a football match. After some name-calling and verbal sparring we discover we are both scouts and class differences melt away.

A while later we had another visitor, this time from the headquarters of Bedfordshire scouting. We assumed it to be an inspection of some sort which in a sense it was, as the visitor was engaged in selecting candidates for the Bedfordshire element of the party of British scouts to attend the first post-war World Jamboree, to be held in France that summer, in August 1946. Two scouts were selected from Luton: I was one, the other a fellow member of the Lower Sixth.

I later received the neckerchief to be worn, an identity card-cum-visa and assembly instructions. In due course I joined the British contingent of several hundred which descended on Moisson in northern France, where a campsite had been prepared for the expected

24,000 visitors from thirty-eight countries. It was a huge undertaking with tents, latrines, water system, and camp stores from which to draw the daily rations which were issued with suggested recipes and warnings for 'Israelites and Mussulmans'.

The sun blazed throughout the day but at nightfall the temperature dropped like a stone and we shivered under our blankets. Wasps were a plague: a spoonful of jam from the jar came with a portion of wasps. Fruit was on sale and grapes were our undoing. An unimagined luxury, there they were for the gorging, bunches heaped up high, costing a pittance. We gobbled the bunch from below like urchin boys in a Velasquez picture and we paid the price. Visiting the latrine was a very un-British experience. The size of the open latrine pit was alarming and, more alarming still, the arrangement of the cubicles. Instead of being on terra firma at the side they were on a sort of bridge structure and swayed up and down.

On the last night there was a big set occasion when all 20,000 scouts assembled in the arena to watch a torchlight procession. The loudspeaker blared out music and greetings to all parts of the world. We joined in tribal chanting:

Massambili bili bili banga, Massambili bili ba
Massambili bil bili banga, Massambili bili ba
Oulanga, Oulanga
Shalliwalli, Walli, Walli, Walli, wa
Oompah, Oompah

The oompahs continued as a drum beat to repetition of the chant. The solemn moment was the singing of the anthem of the Jamboree, a song about youth and unity in those heady post-war years: 'Si tous les gars et filles du monde/ formaient lys d'or/ au noeud d'argent' – 'if all the boys and girls of the world formed the golden fleur de lis with silver knot', the emblem of the Jamboree. Finally, we marched off into the night chanting ajiji ajiji aa oo aa….

Switzerland and climbing

The Jamboree was not the only event of that August. The first post-war overseas school visit took place on dates which to my great relief did not clash with the Jamboree. We were invited to choose between Lugano and Montreux in Switzerland and chose Montreux. I expect my parents put up the money and, to my surprise, Father Brewer, the parish priest, gave me £5 pocket money, a not inconsiderable sum in those days.

As a member of the choir, I saw him frequently and over time became more at ease with this large and ungainly man who with his gold-rimmed glasses looked like Pope Pius XI. He let more of his inner self show. He was proud of his breath control. At choir practices he emphasised its importance and claimed that he could sing the whole of one verse of Adoro Te in one breath. At Benediction one day, he attempted this feat and sought out my eye as his strangled voice died to a choking whisper on the last word. Watching him awkwardly trying to make conversation with Mrs McCullough, her latest baby sliding off her lap, I wondered how this intellectual man, ordained by the Pope after training at the English College in Rome, viewed his fate stuck on the fringes of Luton in a church with a corrugated iron roof.

With the extra £5 in my pocket I assembled with the rest of the party at Luton station. The first part of the journey was by train to Newhaven, which involved crossing London from St Pancras to Victoria Station to connect with the onward train. At St Pancras, I was approached by a classmate who was not part of my group of friends but who was to play a major role in my life. This was David Atkinson. We had come up through the school in the same class but I had never had anything to do with him. He had no profile of achievement in examinations, he did not belong to any clique and was reserved and secretive. I could not recall ever having spoken to him and only really knew of him as the fly-half of the school First XV.

I was therefore surprised and a little flattered when, on arrival at St Pancras, he sought me out and suggested that we race across London to be the first to arrive at Victoria. It was a purely imaginary competition as there was plenty of time and no challengers but I fell in with his proposal. In later years he told me that he had selected me to be his companion in the adventures he hoped to get up to in Switzerland on account of my prowess in cross country.

Mr Parry, a multi-talented teacher who primarily taught RI but could turn his hand to maths and geography, was in charge of the party. We reached Paris as the light was fading and, with plenty of time before our onward train, Mr Parry took us for a meal. We followed him, excited, through the busy streets to a cafe near the Gare St Lazare into which, after a cautionary check by Mr Parry, we all trooped, goggling at the men in berets and blue overalls drinking wine at the bar. In this den of vice, a waiter in a long white apron settled us at pulled-together tables and Mr Parry ordered food. In his choice of drink, with a wink and a knowing look, he led us further into the depths of depravity: he ordered Vichy water with its sulphurous taste of hell.

We travelled overnight from the Gare de Lyon and, opening our eyes in Montreux, the contrast with Luton was so extreme that we thought that we had somehow gone to heaven. In the cool morning air the lake lay blue and placid, a castle at its side and snow-capped mountains beyond. After a hurried breakfast at the hotel we unpacked our swimming things and raced down to the lake.

Atkinson was unexpectedly a lively companion. He had lots of ideas about what to do, tricks to play, always determined to be different and to undermine order. There were two planned excursions, the first of which was a visit to the Grand St Bernard Pass by bus. On arrival we were told that we had two hours at our disposal and, instead of looking at dogs or monks, at Atkinson's suggestion we shot up the mountainside, aiming for the summit. It was far out of reach and, carelessly and perhaps deliberately, we misjudged the time at our disposal. A very angry Mr Parry was waiting for us; because of our irresponsibility the bus had missed its slot in the up/down timetable.

The second excursion was a trip up the cog-railway to the summit of the Rochers-de-Naye, a 6,000 ft mountain behind Montreux. From the station at the top, a path winds its way to the summit. Needless to say, we did not take the path. Atkinson insisted that we take a direct line up the grass slope which was steep enough to need support from the hands. We had not gone far before I regretted not having taken the path as the soles of my sandals, polished by the dry wiry grass, had lost their grip. Retreat was uninviting and, hoping for the best, I clawed my way up to the final turn of the summit path at which point fear gave way to elation. This and the climb at the St Bernard Pass created an appetite for more, and I agreed to Atkinsons' suggestion that on return home we hitch-hike to Skye to climb the Cuillin Ridge.

We put this ambitious plan into effect. We travelled light; we had ex-Army anoraks and trousers bought from a shop in Luton, odds and ends of clothing and washing gear carried in ex-Army frame rucksacks. I wore a pair of ex-Army boots loaned by the Scoutmaster which more or less fitted. We did not take any camping gear and did not then possess any climbing equipment. We got short lifts by drivers curious to know what these sixteen-year-old boys were up to and, late at night, a dream lift, a lone driver heading for Edinburgh in his new American car collected that day from Southampton. At 5am we were walking up a deserted Princes Street. The bus to Queensferry put us back on the road north and by nightfall we were at Atkinson's maternal aunt's house on the southern shore of Loch Ness.

We spent three nights at Glen Nevis Youth Hostel and trudged up to the summit of Ben Nevis. Before leaving Fort William for Mallaig, in an act of exuberant and self-deceiving folly, we sent an unsigned telegram to the Headmaster who was on holiday in Mallaig. We knew he was staying at the hotel run by relatives of a school friend (my fellow correspondent with the Pope) who was also staying there on holiday and was to come with us to Skye. The text of our smarty and unimaginative telegram was 'Help! My grandmother's ear trumpet has been struck by lightning'. Any despairing hope that the Headmaster would not put two and two together was dashed by his frosty greeting and assurance that his grandmother's trumpet was undamaged.

On Skye, we were going to self-cater at the youth hostel to keep costs down and so provisioned ourselves in Mallaig. We bought potatoes, unaware that they could be bought at the hostel, and to go with them several tins of Kitty Kat, a tin of Bournvita and, for variety, a small tin of anchovy fillets. Over the sea to Skye we went and trudged down Glen Brittle in the rain. The hostel was warm and steamy and sitting at tables, wet clothing over the back of their chairs, were serious men with shaggy hair and beards, oiling wet boots. Wet and bedraggled though we were after the long walk, we merited no more than a passing glance from these hard men. After one night our companion, a self-proclaimed aesthete, decided to return to Mallaig unable to face the prospect of confinement to the hostel with only cat food for dinner. We climbed up and explored the famous Cuillin Ridge on eight of the nine days of our stay in more or less continuous rain, so wet that the upper of one of the Scoutmaster's boots came away from the sole. For a treat on our last night we opened the tin of anchovies but, not liking their taste, gave them to the hard men.

The hitch-hike back to Luton was laborious. One lift left us at Ballachulish and, bored after waiting a long time, we decided to walk on as we would not miss any potential lift. Night fell and we found ourselves stranded in the rain on Rannoch Moor. After an age, headlights appeared and we presented so piteous a spectacle that the car stopped and took us the many remaining miles to the King's House Hotel and left us there. What to do? We had no money. We went in and before we could begin to explain our predicament we were shushed away to bed with milk and biscuits. The following morning our explanation was anticipated: 'you'll no doubt be sending us the money when you get back home'.

I saw a lot of Atkinson outside school, spending time at each other's house. My mother did not take to him at all. He did not hold her eye. She found him sly and secretive and regarded him as an altogether bad influence. This was all true, as I well knew, and worse than Mother suspected as he was subversive and dangerous, but I was along for the ride. Our scrambles in the Alps and on Skye created an appetite for yet more and we planned to go to North Wales in the Easter holidays for our first rock climbs.

We read up all the climbing literature we could find and, following the advice in J E Q Barford's book, Climbing in Britain, bought 120 feet of manila hemp rope from a ships' chandler in the London docks, but lacked the nerve to assure ourselves of its quality by twisting open the rope and sniffing it, as recommended. For our boots, we went to Robert Lawrie, outfitter to the discerning climber. He ran his business from the sitting room of his house near Marble Arch. He gave us his full attention as if we were embarked on some mighty endeavour. Our feet were measured and boots brought to try on while grave, silent men stood around examining crampons or were locked in conversation with Mr Lawrie about the quality of Italian ice-axes. When it came to the nailing pattern for our boots, however, we knew our stuff and, though we had absolutely no practical experience, specified the nails and the arrangement required.

We bought the guidebooks for Ogwen and Glyder Fach. These listed and graded the known climbs in the area at the time and were the work of two climbers, Menlove Edwards and Colin Kirkus, who dominated climbing exploration in the pre-war years. In the 1940s, rock climbing was picking up after the war. There had been a few new routes put up during the war by exceptionally fit soldiers and there was talk of happenings in the Llanberis Pass, but the Joe Brown era and the explosion of climbing lay ten years ahead. As we were to find, there were relatively few climbers around and those at Ogwen congregated at Mervyn's tea shack, a shed attached to the rear of the wall by the side of the road, to linger over a cup of tea before setting off to climb. Climbers know this as 'festering', a form of guilty idleness charged with anticipation.

We had our first sight of Tryfan as the bus from Bangor rounded a bend on approaching Ogwen. The whole mountain suddenly came into view, shimmering in a purple haze, heart-stopping, irresistible. We threw down our sacks and raced across to the west face, ignoring paths, and scrambled up to the summit. On the succeeding days we climbed, rain or shine, our nailed boots unaffected by the wet. We started with the easiest climb in the guidebook and, working our way up through Difficult and Very Difficult routes, climbed a Severe on our fourth day. The leader climbed unprotected in those days; there was none of the panoply of safety devices available today. Your only equipment was the rope: you tied it round your waist, you belayed yourself at the stance with it and you brought your second up with it. It was no help to you if you fell.

In succeeding school holidays, we returned to Wales and, as our confidence grew, climbed ever harder routes. Somewhat to my surprise, I was bolder than Atkinson and many of the Severe climbs I led effectively solo are today graded Very Severe, but the real heart-stopping moments occur when least expected, on an 'easy' climb facing a long reach over hair-raising exposure.

We bought ice-axes and during the Christmas holidays hitch-hiked to Wales hoping for climbable snow. For extra warmth, I wore a waistcoat I had made out of a child's overcoat with the sleeves ripped off. In dog-tooth check and with a string fastening, it created quite a stir at Capel Curig Youth Hostel where we stayed and it became a trademark. To enliven the evenings, Atkinson and I put on our own Gang Show with round songs and sketches from Baden-Powell's Scouting for Boys. Atkinson wore big pushed-down socks and so successful were we that the warden asked the Sox and Waistcoat duo to stay on. Enough was enough.

School – the later years

After that action-packed summer, we returned to school very pleased with ourselves and progressed with the class to the heights of the Upper Sixth. Academically, the year unfolded without incident and at its end I took the Higher School Certificate examination not too concerned about the result, regarding it as a trial run for next year's final push. I became a prefect, captain of Cross-Country and, to the bemusement of staff as I was an arts student, chairman of the Biology Club. Among the outings I organised were an eye and breath-catching visit to the sewage farm and a hostelling weekend by bicycle to Felixstowe to examine the life of the seashore. All but four of the party were too tired even to go down to the beach and spent the day returning by train.

Our last year at school arrived with the class reduced to those intending to go on to university. Three of us went to Cambridge for scholarship exams in October and were lodged in Jesus College in cold rooms off a stone staircase opening onto a courtyard. My heart swelled; it was all I had imagined. As the University was down it was quiet, and walking at night in dimly-lit streets past ancient colleges I imagined Cambridge in medieval times. However, imagination did not produce results and I returned from Cambridge empty handed. I would have to find another way to get there.

In the summer term I got into serious trouble as the result of a cheeky answer. The class was rehearsing its unexciting contribution to the school gym display, a marching routine, under the direction of the gym master. I was at the head of one line. The order to halt was given on my deaf side and by the time I registered it I had walked on a few paces. The gym master called out 'are you deaf?' and I fell into the trap of saying 'yes'. He beckoned me over and said, 'Do you know what's going to happen to you now?' He swung his arm back and clouted me on the ear with such force that I staggered and when I recovered myself he struck again. My fellows were silent, school was pouring out for break and could see what happened, a prefect receiving blows from a master.

In the afternoon, I was summoned by the Headmaster and found the Head Boy sitting with him. The Headmaster asked if I wished to make a complaint, and if I did, I should be aware that it would cost the master his job. If I had been asked the following day I would probably have said 'no,' but I was still so highly charged that I said 'yes'. That was my undoing. Though the gym master was well known by the boys to have a quick temper and to strike out and though the school was well rid of him, I was the one who got him the sack. My relationship with three of my teachers appeared not to change but the main two, the French and Spanish masters, made it clear that they did not wish to have anything further to do with me. I did not tell my parents about the incident or its sequel; I was ashamed of my behaviour and, in any case, I knew they would be too timid to do anything about it.

Within days I had an accident. A number of us were taking part in a course run by the AA outside school hours to teach young men to ride motorbikes safely. We had progressed through lessons about safety, the parts of the motorbike, sitting on one going through the motions, and were finally going to have our first ride in a private park. Hitherto bravado had kept me going as I felt physically unequal to handling the motorbike and when my turn came I crossed my fingers. After a smooth start I changed gear and was away accelerating, then braking and changing down for a corner when it all went wrong. From such recall as I have, I failed to engage the gear and the bike began to shake uncontrollably. I lost control and was found, after I failed to return, unconscious. No helmets in those days.

I came to in hospital with Mother at the bedside. She said she had had a premonition that something would go wrong when I put on a new shirt which was now ruined. I had cracked my skull. It was no comfort to know that the course had been cancelled and that my accident was the first ever on this AA course. After a week or more I was discharged and all seemed normal until I found that reading brought on an intense and persistent headache which made return to school pointless. By the time the headache eased I had lost so much time that, with the end of term approaching, I decided to absent myself for the rest of it. I thus missed my second attempt at the Higher School Certificate examination.

I devoted myself to work in the garden of our new council house. It literally was new, one of an estate built on high ground on the fringe of Luton across the hill from Percival Aircraft, the site today of Luton Airport. The semi-detached house was prefabricated and had the usual utilitarian appearance but inside it was a wonder. The floors downstairs were composed of a shiny mastic, warm to the touch and, in the front room, there was an efficient coke-burning fire which heated water that also fed a couple of radiators. How we came to be offered this marvellous house, said to be of Swedish design, is a mystery and I can only think it was due to Mother pestering the council.

Before the dramas at school, I had arranged with my two closest friends to go on a cycling holiday in France in the summer holidays staying at youth hostels. In late August, we met at the ferry terminal in Newhaven and crossed to Dieppe. By the time we got clear with our ration cards it was late to be setting off on the sixty-mile ride to Rouen, our first stop, eventually arriving after nightfall. We found the hostel in some disorder. Cooking was on a wood-burning range and laths were being pulled down from the ceiling to stoke the fire.

The late arrival set a daily routine we seemed unable to correct: late arrival, late departure, late arrival again after cycling through the heat of the day. However, it had advantages. In the lazy mornings we could look around and enjoy being in France and buy our baguette, tomatoes and camembert for lunch which we usually ate halfway through the afternoon. The further we progressed south, the more the journey itself became our chief preoccupation and when we entered the hilly country of the Massif Central the going became hard. After a laborious day on the comparatively short distance between Gueret and Ussel, we admitted defeat. Our ambition to reach the Mediterranean was beyond us and it was time to turn back.

We had come a good way south as Ussel lies due west of Lyon and, rather than retrace our route, we headed east to pick up the arterial road to the north, catching sight of the Alps in the far distance. Our only interest now was to get back. We looped round Paris to the east and, late in the afternoon of 11th September, we were in Dieppe once more after sixteen days having covered a thousand miles and more. We landed at Newhaven in heavy rain on the blackest of nights and were led by a policeman to somewhere to stay. In the morning, my two companions took the train. I like to think that I cycled back to Luton but, as I have no memory of so doing, I suspect I threw in the towel and went with them.

My friends were not under any time pressure as they had left school and were awaiting call-up for National Service. For my part I faced a further year at school but, having failed the Army medical on account of my hearing, I had a year in hand and could remain in step with my peers. As I anticipated, my late return to school aroused no comment. The attitude of the staff was a weary 'so you're back again'. There was no change in the attitude of the Spanish and French masters who, while ignoring me, had to put up with my presence in the classroom as there was nowhere else for me to go. Though sharing the classroom with the Second Year Upper Sixth, I was not a member of the class so I had no out-of-classroom base and could not use the Prefects' Common room as I had effectively ceased to be a Prefect. I inhabited a no man's land.

Outside school I reached the pinnacle of my Scout career. I finally completed the marathon of qualifications required for King's Scout. The presentation of the award took place in London. On the eve of the ceremony scouts from all over the country assembled at Captain Scott's ship, the Discovery, moored in the Thames and, after the night on board, we were taken to one of the nearby Inns of Court to receive our certificates from Lord Rowallan, the Chief Scout.

I ploughed my lonely furrow at school and in the Higher School Certificate examination at the end of the summer term I obtained the highest marks in French and Spanish. Prizes were given out on Speech Day but as I was abroad mine were sent by post, not two, but the French prize only as the Spanish master had put his best student up for the prize for Spanish. I pointed this out and the matter was rectified. Though the prizes were a consolation, once again I had not done as well as I had hoped. I had fallen just short of obtaining the distinctions needed to qualify for a State Scholarship. I performed inexplicably badly in one paper and in normal circumstance it might have been reviewed but, as it was, I had to be content with a place on the reserve list.

An extra page was fixed in my report book and the final report gave no indication of my trials and tribulations. It was as if nothing had happened. All the masters wrote well of my work including the French and Spanish masters, despite their not having set any. The Headmaster's valedictory report, too, was generous. It reads:

> R A McDonald leaves us a vigorous, athletic, mature young man of considerable ability, fluency in two modern languages, and displaying marked initiative and independence. There have been times when I have thought he was too impetuous and unthoughtful, but though the spirit of adventure is still strong in him, he has grown less hasty. With his alert and cheerful disposition, native wit and intelligence and sound physique, he should enjoy the happiness and success we wish for him.

That however was not the end of the story. Years later, when taking leave of the Tutor at the end of my time at Cambridge, I asked why the College had accepted me, an unsupported applicant with moderate academic achievement. He said it was due to your Headmaster. We asked him about you and when he replied that you had scant respect for authority and were the type likely to indulge in night-climbing, we knew we would have to have you.

Iceland

In July 1949, I at last finished with school and Atkinson was at the end of his first year at Imperial College. We had been wondering about how and where to spend the summer and Atkinson proposed Iceland, emboldened by his experience in Canada the previous summer as a member of a Public Schools Expedition. It was a typically ambitious idea and an exciting prospect. The stories of Scott and Shackleton and The Worst Journey in the World were rooted in my imagination and I longed to experience the snow, the ice, the remote empty spaces. Iceland was not the Antarctic, but it was a step in that direction.

We both felt equal to the challenges Iceland might present and not in the least daunted. We had by then done quite a lot of climbing. We had been to Wales three times, hitchhiking, sleeping rough and climbing in bad conditions. We had even tried bivouacking without shelter, sharing one sleeping bag. The sheer craziness of the idea appealed to us. We reclined on a heap of gravel beside the road in North Wales and, with the bag worked up to chest level, endured the passage of the night hours, unable to find any comfortable position for our arms, indeed hardly able to move at all.

We learned about Iceland from a book written by a traveller in the 1920s and we studied the map. Of obvious interest was the icecap of

Vatnajokull, which covers eleven per cent of Iceland's land area, but getting to it looked problematic and we had no ice experience. The description of Askja, 5,000 ft high, with its huge crater and turquoise-blue lake in the heart of a lava desert, caught our imagination. It was accessible from the north and had moreover a legend according to which the lake was bewitched and turned mad those who peered into its depths. Now this looked very promising. We settled on Askja as our goal.

We got ourselves organised. We had our climbing kit and all we needed was a sleeping bag for me and a small tent. Atkinson swore by the kapok-filled bag he had used in Canada and, though unimpressed by its performance in the bivouac experiment, I bought a similar one. From an Army surplus store, we bought an ex-US Army bivouac tent consisting of two lengths of canvas that buttoned together to form the ridge of the tent and two little wooden supporting poles. When erected, the tent was so low and narrow that the only way to enter it was to shuffle in backwards. For a groundsheet, we bought ex-military dual-purpose gas capes. These were oblongs of camouflaged rubberized fabric with a collar arrangement on one side.

We modelled our rations on those of Atkinson's Canada expedition, the centrepiece of which was tinned cheese. We would have cheese and ships' biscuits for lunch and again for dinner, with porridge for breakfast and, to keep our spirits high, a small amount of chocolate. Though more palatable than cat food and mash it was not much to look forward to, but food was the least of our concerns. All hinged on getting to Iceland in the first place. Our plan was to hitchhike on a trawler and, with no idea how this might be achieved, we set off for Grimsby with our kit, dressed for Iceland and with a few pounds in our pockets.

Walking from Grimsby station we quickly tired of carrying the box containing the overflow from the rucksacks. What we needed was something on wheels onto which we could transfer our entire load, a kind of land sledge, and passing a junkyard we went in out of curiosity. Remarkably we found a pair of pram wheels on axles and with the enthusiastic help of the junkyard man our trolley took shape. Two boards of wood were found to which to bolt the axles and, thinking further ahead, I saw that the trolley could be converted into a makeshift sledge by bolting the axles to the edge of the boards and had one end of them cut in a curve. Towing this dual-purpose contraption, we continued towards the docks.

Every step brought us closer to the daunting task ahead and our confidence began to sag. How do you go about hitching a lift on a trawler? Would we even be allowed on the dockside? We plodded on in a subdued mood. A man leaning in a doorway called out as we passed 'Hello boys. Are you Bevin Boys?' alluding to conscripts sent down the mines rather than to the Services. In the ensuing conversation we told him what we hoped to do. He said, 'Do you know anybody?' and, after the negative answer, continued 'I might be able to help you.' He invited us in to have something to eat and as we ate from the plate of cold battered fish on the table, men stopped by and dealt briefly with our host who explained that he was a bookmaker. When we were ready to move, he gave us instructions: 'Find Chris Ottosan's fish and chip shop in the harbour, tell him what you want to do and tell him that I sent you.'

We trundled down to the docks and introduced ourselves to Mr Ottosan in his fish and chip shop and told him our story. 'Okay' he said, 'have you eaten?' Never declining food, we ate our way through a large helping of fish and chips after which he took us over to meet his brother, or cousin or relative of his, the editor of a newspaper in Reykjavik. In response to his questions, we described our plan to go to Askja, ideally from the northern port of Akureyri, and thereafter make our way to Reykjavik and from there visit the tourist sites of Geysir and Gullfoss and finally Hekla which, a year after its eruption, might be approachable. 'When you get to Reykjavik,' our new editor friend said, 'come and see me straight away.'

A further surprise lay in store. Mr Ottosan asked where we were staying that night and, having anticipated our reply, said that we could sleep on his boat in the harbour. Later in the evening, the boat's night-watchman shepherded us down to the quayside and rowed us across to a small fishing boat. We sat up late listening to the gnarled old seaman saying over and over when conversation dried up, 'They're grand little boats, these, but they need pumping.' Leaving him to his pumping, we went to bed marvelling at the turn of events and wondering what hold the bookmaker had on the Ottosan family. Though no one had said as much, it was implicit that we were on our way to Iceland.

In the morning, we were rowed back to the quayside and directed to a large new-looking ship taking on ice which rattled down the chute into the hold. We went on board and eventually, in that slow-motion time peculiar to ships, we put to sea, destination Akureyri. What concatenation of good fortune! With our hearts singing, we stood on the high prow of the trawler as it plunged into the North Sea. Before long, the rise and fall of the ship, at its most exaggerated on the prow, and the piercing wind drove us below where we surrendered to seasickness. We lay there watching the curtains of the bunk rise and fall as if by magic as the boat rolled from side to side. The nausea passed and a day later we went on deck to see the Faroe Islands floating past, rich brown cliffs with foam at their feet and brilliant green fields above. Behind us, keeping pace with the trawler, fulmar petrels hung motionless in the air.

We landed at Akureyri on the 1st of August and on going ashore were scooped up by the Mission to Seamen before we had time to think what to do next. Unresisting, we were led by Arthur Gook, in charge of the Mission, to the Mission House where we stayed for a couple of days, attending morning and evening prayers, while we made ready for our journey to Askja. In town we were stopped by a man who said in anguished tones, 'You must not go to Askja. It is too strong for you.' Word of our intentions had evidently got around. Was he alluding to the Curse of the Lake?

The first stage of the journey was to Myvatn, a large lake, forty-five miles east of Akureyri. We set off with the Pride of Grimsby, our trolley, only to find it a liability. The load, though reduced to the two rucksacks with fifteen days food, was still heavy enough to drive the thin pram wheels into the crushed and rolled lava of the road surface, making the trolley hard to pull. It had had its day: the trolley had to go. We hid it some distance from the road as best we could in the sparse vegetation and, shouldering our sacks, walked on. A car approached. We thumbed it; it stopped and out tumbled sailors from the trawler. They were in high spirits and high on spirits and soon we were passing a bottle of gin round. When it was empty, they shook our hands and drove off leaving us staggering in the road. I swung my rucksack up onto my shoulder and fell flat on my back. We slept a while by the side of the road.

We spent our first night under canvas at Myvatn, translation Fly Lake, not unduly troubled by flies. The lake teemed with ducks and waders while plovers scurried round in the dwarf willows on its shores. The route to Askja lay south over the Odadahraun, the grey lava desert formed of layer upon layer of lava flows which stretched all the way to the Vatnajokull icecap. At grips at last with the central purpose of our venture, we were surprised at the end of the first day's march to see in the distance a building which, on approaching, seemed to be a farmhouse, though what it farmed was not evident as the desert was bare of vegetation. My Icelandic phrase book contained the words for 'sleep', 'in' and 'barn' and with 'sova i hlada' on my lips I knocked on the door. The lady who opened it was surprised to see us and, whatever she made of what I had said, invited us in. We were plied first with pastries to satiety and, after a long, long wait, a plate of boiled lamb and vegetables was set before us. All this time we were left alone in the sitting room and we ate alone. We were later led to a bedroom where a bed with sheets awaited. The hospitality was far beyond any expectation and as the lady of the house appeared to have no English, or not to wish to use it, we could not fully communicate our appreciation and felt very awkward. We did not see any menfolk.

The following day we were again surprised to come upon a dwelling in the wilderness and it all happened again. Clearly forewarned, our new hosts were waiting for us and before I could utter 'sova i hlada' they welcomed us in. Events unfolded as in the previous day and so it was, yet again, on the following day as we reached the third of these outposts in the desert. Our host spoke excellent English and surrounded by his books he had the air of a scholarly recluse. His special interest was the ecology of the desert and he pressed us to stay for a second day to make a botanical foray to a nearby area which supported some vegetation. We fell in with his proposal and on return from our foray he examined and named the little we had found: lichens of varying colours, some species of grass and our prize, the small, fleshy veined leaves of a plant which he identified as dryas octopetala, the mountain avens. He showed us a picture of the plant with its eight-petalled flower, the national emblem of Iceland. I have since always looked out for this unobtrusive plant, my Iceland trophy, and have found it at levels up to 10,000 ft.

We had arrived within striking distance of Askja, unexpectedly well fed and housed but with blisters on our heels and swellings like knots in the Achilles tendon, presumably caused by walking over the broken ground with our sacks. Atkinson had packed a small bottle of tincture of iodine which proved remarkably effective in drying up burst blisters, while the knots in the tendon, we found, could be massaged away. We performed these excruciating procedures simultaneously on each other, lying head to foot, heedless of the suffering caused.

We marched on to Askja and climbed to the rim of the vast crater, five miles wide, and saw in the distance the enchanted lake. This was what we had come to see and we savoured our moments of triumph before scrambling down the thousand-foot wall to the floor of the crater to find somewhere to pitch our tent amid the jagged black lava. The sky was overcast, and it was cold. After yet more cheese and biscuits we wriggled into the tent and into our sleeping bags. The thin gas-cape groundsheet provided no comfort or insulation and the heat generated by our bodies was lost because of the inadequate closure of the tent. We slept fitfully, waking up shivering. I found that crouching on my knees and elbows was the warmest position. The kapok sleeping bag went down further in my estimation.

We did not have enough water to make porridge and so, after cheese and biscuits for breakfast, we set off with our water bottles to fill them at the lake. Picking our way through the chaotic lava was entertaining to begin with but became tedious with the need to tread carefully to avoid shredding our boots on the sharp lava. The huge lake, more than two miles across, was not turquoise or blue of any kind, just grey under a grey sky. We peered intently into its depths without becoming any madder than we already were and filled the water bottles taking care not to fall in and drown, the presumed fate of two German scientists visiting Askja in 1907, the source of the legend.

Back at the tent, now what? We had seen what we had come to see and a further night was uninviting so we packed up the tent, climbed to the rim of the crater and, after a last look back, set off down. We did not return via the homesteads but struck off in a direct line towards Myvatn veering east to the Jokulsa, the river flowing north from Vatnajokull. Walking along the bank of the river we began to have fantasies about food. Each of us in turn would describe in detail a meal of great length and quantity, lingering over each item, a breakfast for instance consisting of orange juice, kippers, bacon, egg, sausage, fried tomato, fried bread, black pudding, baked beans, buttered toast, marmalade, tea and coffee. The meal chosen was nearly always breakfast, each striving to outdo the other, both speaker and listener deadly serious. In three days we reached the road to the east of Myvatn and hitchhiked back to the Seaman's Mission where the food fantasies evaporated. Picking up the food we had left behind we set off for Reykjavik. The worthy Mr Gook had a parting gift for us, two pamphlets written by him, 'Seen by Angels' price tuppence and 'Can a Young Man Overcome?' price fourpence, which we received with becoming gravity.

The road to Reykjavik ran for 250 miles round the western coast of the island. We got there in two lifts and as instructed reported to the newspaper editor. Reminded of the tourist sites we hoped to see, he telephoned the Director of Tourism and sent us round to see him. He had bus tickets to Geysir and Gullfoss ready for us, and as we turned to leave, he asked where we would be staying and, to our reply that we would find somewhere to camp, said 'you'd better stay at the Airport Hotel'. Why was all this happening to us? It was as if a fairy queen was hovering over us and at every check waved her magic wand.

The manager of the hotel stopped us when we walked into the dining room, asking if it was agreed that food was included and, when we could not answer his question, went away to telephone. He came back and waved us forward, visibly unhappy. To keep out of his sight we set off the following morning on our travels. Geysir was a disappointment. The mud bubbled and glugged and tried but could not find the puff for its famed 200-feet high spurt. On to Gullfoss, the Golden Falls. We watched the cascading waters for a while then, separating from the bus party, headed off in the direction of Hekla, walking and hitching as usual. At one point, we came to a fast-flowing river. How to get across? We enquired at a farm nearby and after a while three Icelandic ponies were led out by a taciturn man. We sat on the ponies bareback, clutching their manes. They waded without hesitation into the water and walking or swimming crossed to the other bank. Our leader did not dismount and, after we had thanked him, led his ponies back across the river.

Hekla, some 5,000 ft high, lay back before us at a gentle angle. The lower slopes were clothed with dwarf birches and willow which thinned out as we ascended. We came eventually to new lava and higher to warm lava as the 1947 eruption had rumbled on for a while. In the jumble of lava, we found somewhere that would do for the night, so warm that neither tent nor sleeping bag was needed. I found a fissure in the lava, a fumarole, out of which a jet of hot air issued and balanced on it the pan with our morning porridge to cook overnight. What more could we want? In the morning we climbed towards the summit in hope of being able to look down into the crater but as we neared the top a gust of wind brought down a cloud of acrid fumes. Time to retreat.

Back at the Airport Hotel a summons awaited us: we were to report to the Consul at the British Embassy. She asked us if it was true that we were staying at the hotel at the expense of the Icelandic Government, as indeed we were. She heard what we had to say and gave us a few days to arrange our departure or face repatriation as Distressed British Subjects. We told our newspaper friend that we had been given marching orders and needed to find work to raise money to pay fares. As always, he picked up the telephone and spoke, this time, to someone in the Ministry of Labour. We then called on the man he had spoken to, whom we believed to be the Minister himself (it could be true!) who, looking out of his window on labourers at work in the street below, arranged for us to join them the following day.

News of our predicament became widely known. At the hotel, one of the guests gave me two presentation sets of pen and propelling pencil to sell to raise money and, astonishingly, we were stopped twice in the street by strangers who gave us money, 50 Krona from a woman and 100 Krona from a man. With this money, the proceeds of the sale of the pen sets to our fellow workers, the wages we earned in four days plus our few remaining pounds, we had enough to take to Icelandic Airways to beg for a reduced-price ticket to Prestwick. Icelandic Airways were generous. They too seemed part of the conspiracy to help us.

We flew to Prestwick on the 20th of September. As soon as we were out of the airport, Atkinson dramatically threw away our remaining money, a sixpence. Money was a constraint, he declared, without it we will be shameless and in this frame of mind we set off on the hitchhike home. We made slow progress and reached Motherwell, twenty-five miles south of Glasgow, at ten o'clock that night. Determined to be shameless, I knocked on a door and found myself asking if there were any crusts we might have. The lady answering the door took a good look at us then asked, 'Where are you from?' Iceland. 'Oh, yes?' she said, disbelieving, and as we made to leave gestured us to sit on the step. She went inside and returned after a while with sandwiches and cocoa.

Taking up position on the road south, we thumbed to no avail and spent the night in the hedge after finally brushing off a man who insisted we go with him to watch his friend who trained in the nude. In the morning we got a short lift to a transport cafe. Once more summoning up my shamelessness, I asked the lady at the counter if there was any work we could do in return for some breakfast and, after similar exchanges to those of the previous evening, we sat down at the table. A lorry driver of her acquaintance came in for his breakfast. She asked him where he was heading that day. Newcastle. 'You'll take these boys, then' she instructed him. We were back home by nightfall and our seven-week visit to Iceland by magic carpet came to its end. A reporter from the Luton News interviewed us and five lines appeared under the headline: 'THEY FOUND HOTSPOTS IN ICELAND.'

Seventy years on, Iceland today is a tourism destination. Visiting Askja is now a three-day 4x4 trip with overnight stays in hostels, perhaps the homesteads we stayed in. There are bird-watching holidays at Myvatn, skiing on Hekla and 4x4 vehicles on the Vatnajokull icecap. How fortunate we were.

Spain

On the 18th of October 1949, nineteen days after returning from Iceland, I set off for Spain. I longed to go there, to see Spain, to put to the test all I had learned, and the fallow months ahead provided the opportunity. Next summer I would go with Atkinson on the Arctic expedition he was planning and thereafter, I hoped, go on to Cambridge but meanwhile I had a good six months at my disposal. To sustain a long stay I would need to find work, and with this in mind I bought a casual suit in a greenish colour in which to make myself respectable. With that and £20 entered in my passport, I waved goodbye.

I decided not to begin hitchhiking from Luton as I could lose days in getting to the Channel ports, so I took the train to Newhaven. On the London to Newhaven leg of the journey I fell into conversation with a young man of my own age. Very affable and companionable, he broke the ice and in no time at all he told me that he was on his way from Ireland to Paris, then added, 'I am a Jew. I hope you don't mind.' Reassured, he went on to explain that his aunt, tired of him hanging round with nothing to do, had packed him off to Paris with £20 in his pocket. We travelled together on the boat, and at Dieppe I allowed myself to be cajoled into taking the train with him to Paris where I firmly took leave of him.

I was cross with myself for having made such a hole in my finances and vowed that there would be no further backsliding. I made painfully slow progress, taking three days to reach Lyon, during which time I lived on bread and tomatoes and slept rough. At Lyon I pampered myself by staying two nights at the youth hostel, glad of the rest and the company. I fell in with a little community of apparently permanent residents who took me for a fellow derelict. We clubbed together to buy the ingredients of some vaunted stew which turned out to be mostly potato and olive oil. Among the merry men was a young Englishman, a student of opera, scraping by on his pay as a sweeper at the Opera House in the hope of attracting a patron. A great moment had arrived: he was invited to a dinner by a lady who had taken an interest in him and we all took a hand in preparing him for the occasion, supervising his shave, tidying up his hair, washing and ironing his shirt, the cuffs of which were so ingrained with dirt that by common accord they were simply cut off.

I wended my way south in fits and starts through Avignon and Nîmes, reaching Sète on the seventh day of my journey. At the youth hostel I met a Belgian who like me was hitching to Spain. We agreed to continue together and three days later we were trudging up the last miles to the Spanish frontier. A gendarme wobbled by on his bicycle. Ten minutes later, the famous predatory Citroën of a thousand flic movies roared up and disgorged its occupants. After a glance at my passport I was waved on but my companion was given the full treatment: he had to strip and the contents of his sack were spread over the road. Finally he was allowed on his way, having persuaded the police that he was not a fugitive Nazi and that his passport and other papers granting him concessions as a former concentration camp victim were genuine. He showed me the number on his arm.

We crossed into Spain at La Jonquera on the 29th of October, eleven days after I had left home. My remaining worldly wealth was entered in my passport: £4 and 120 francs. We were now in Franco Spain, ten years after the Civil War and four years after the Second World War, but there was no sense of repression at the frontier and without interference we eventually got a lift to Barcelona, a distance of a hundred miles. As we drove in towards the centre of the city, the driver asked where we would be staying. I said that we had nothing decided and would sleep rough if need be. 'No, no, no,' said our driver, 'you would be arrested as vagrants and get yourselves into a lot of trouble. I have an idea.' He pulled up in front of an impressive building and got out to speak with a young man on his way in. He came back and said that this young man would help us. We were thus delivered into the hands of the Falange Youth Movement, the Spanish equivalent of the Hitler Youth.

After brief introductions, we were led into the building and towards the dining room when our companion stopped and remembered that ties were compulsory. I rummaged in my rucksack and brought forth the two ties I had borrowed from my father. We had a frugal and novel meal: the first course included chickpeas and raw green peppers, neither of which I had seen before, and for dessert we ate dried figs. With little Spanish, the Belgian took no part in the conversation in which, as might be expected, our host extolled Franco and his achievements.

After the meal, our young Falangista asked where we were staying and, on hearing that we had no plan, said that he had a Swiss friend who could give us a bed. The Swiss friend welcomed us, gave us coffee and we sat talking, mostly in German and mostly over my head, so I left them to it and went to bed only to be roused by the Belgian who could not wait till morning to tell me that he suspected our host to be German, not Swiss.

The next day we each went to visit our respective Consulates, agreeing to re-gather at lunchtime at the apartment. I hoped that the Consulate could help me find work as I had decided not to press on further into Spain. Barcelona was not the destination I sought as it was not in Spanish Spain, but I had little money left and the warnings about vagrancy could not be ignored. The Consulate proved barren of ideas but, by chance, a teacher from the British Council was also visiting the Consulate. He told me that there was no vacancy at the

Council and suggested that I try my luck at Estudios Friedendorff, a commercial language school, the address of which he gave me.

On return to the flat I found the Belgian beside himself with anxiety. All his papers had disappeared to the feigned astonishment of our Swiss host. The Belgian returned to the Consulate to report the loss and was given the apparently senseless instruction to go back and check again. He did so and found his papers stacked on the top of his rucksack, confirming the Consulate's assumption that they had been taken away to be photographed. We took leave of our host, who barefacedly expressed pleasure that the Belgian had found his mislaid papers, and made our way to the address given by the Belgian Consulate of a Belgian widow who ran a small 'pension'.

The Belgian widow, whom I came to know simply as Madame, was a large untidy woman with fair hair and a brawny arm who ran her business in an apartment in a low-rise building on the outskirts of Barcelona. Apart from rooms for herself and her ten-year-old daughter she had three rooms to let out: one occupied by me for the whole of my stay in Barcelona, one by a young Spaniard of my own age and the third, briefly, by the Belgian who soon went on his way. It was a miracle that she could feed us at all on the one peseta a day she charged. However the meals were consequently of diet proportions which left me unsatisfied as I was skeletal after the journey.

The young Spaniard, Manolo or Manuel Garcia Roman to give him his full name, and I became close friends after some initial sparring. I found him touchy and proud and he found me likewise, mistaking my reserve as typical of the self-assumed superiority of the British. He claimed to be descended from the Duke of Medina Sidonia, the Commander of the Spanish Armada. I made no answer to that. Having taken stock of each other we got on very well; he worked on my Spanish and I helped him with French which he practised on Madame. Manolo introduced me to his friends, one of whom, after hearing me speak, began 'my dear Calderon', a reference to the Golden Age dramatist, which gives an idea of the flavour of my school Spanish. I went to the bullfight with them with some trepidation.

The spectacle of the opening parade was all I hoped for: the raucous trumpets and the toreros in pink and green and gold strutting with that curious pin-toed gait as if their shoes pinched. Their courage and daring had to be admired but it was a long sad spectacle. It had to be seen but once was enough.

Estudios Friedendorff occupied one floor of a building near the Plaza de Catalunya. Spick and span in my green suit I presented myself to Señor Friedendorff, a very tall man with glasses and a brooding presence. He spoke English slowly and carefully with a German accent. Yes, he could give me work, two classes, perhaps more later, thirty pesetas per month per class. First I had to observe the Friedendorff Method, a system of his own invention, in action, and was to come back the following day to attend the class of Dr Smith, a South African, with not one but two Doctorates. I left the building walking on air.

I sat at the back of Dr Dr Smith's class, the Friedendorff Method text-book in my hand, to watch him at work. He was teaching the interrogative of the future in English. The technique was to write the Spanish form of the verb on the blackboard and then invite a member of the class to come up and write the English translation. The first one to do so wrote, translating literally, 'will come he?' and the next 'will sing we?' and so on. I could not bear to remain silent and gave examples of correct usage. Looking sternly at me, Dr Dr Smith said, 'Ja, ja, that you can say.'

There was one other English member of staff, and from him I learned that all the other teachers were German under a variety of English names. Indeed, his own name had been changed for presentational reasons from Verdasco to Verdish. Of Spanish descent, he was the son of a Covent Garden trader and, as far as I could make out, was in Spain to broaden his experience as he had perfect Spanish. We talked about Friedendorff, said to be a White Russian, who could not fail to be aware that, at the very least, he was assisting the exfiltration of fugitive Germans. During my time, Dr Dr Smith himself disappeared. According to one account, he had been arrested and handed over; more likely it was his turn for the boat to South America.

I was, thus, the only teacher at school operating under his own name. I enjoyed my teaching. One class was the individual tuition of a lady in her middle years, exquisitely dressed and groomed and charm itself. She did not, however, have a capacious mind and we never progressed beyond Lesson Two. She enjoyed rattling through 'I am, you are', pronounced 'yam yo-arry', and the verb 'to have' with harsh aitches. We played the Friedendorff Method game in which a pencil is held up and the question posed 'is this a book?'. Confused, she usually got it wrong: 'no, it is a book', pronounced 'bog'.

The other class was the complete opposite, made up of lively people in their twenties and thirties who already had a lot of English and were keen to progress. Reading a passage which contained the sentence 'it is very foggy in Cambridge', the class burst out laughing and explained that they heard the 'g' as a 'k'. To answer some of their questions, for instance on usage of 'may and might' and 'will and shall', I had to do some rapid thinking.

Friedendorff had me broadcast readings to students awaiting classes in the reception area. I adopted a slow sonorous delivery in BBC English and I think it was through these broadcasts that I unconsciously discarded the remnants of Liverpudlian in my speech, the pronunciation of 'hair' and 'fair' as 'her' and 'fur'. At Christmas, my charming pupil gave me a box of goodies which included a packet of tea, and the lively class a handsome Don Quijote which all signed and is to this day on my bookshelf.

I had to do something about my place at Cambridge. I selected as my target Magdalene College, one of the group of colleges for which I had sat the Scholarship Examinations and where the French Oral test had taken place. Conducting the oral had been Dr Ladborough, a Fellow of the College, a most genial man, and in my letter I brazenly made much of the impression he had made on me. In addition to my Highers results, I described all my travels, past, present, and future and in conclusion asked for a quick reply which I learned years later had taken the College aback by its effrontery. After an agonising wait, a letter arrived offering me a place. The letter was addressed to Barcelona, Portugal, which astonished Manolo but which I, safe in possession of my place, attributed to quaint donnish aberration.

Barcelona was very quiet. Only the Ramblas with its profusion of flowers conveyed any sense of busyness. The great central square, the Plaza de Catalunya, had a couple of modish cafes but was usually deserted. There was no visible repression, more a sense of restraint, of order strictly maintained. The Guardia Civil, in their sage green uniforms and strange black helmets, patrolled impassively in pairs ready to pounce on those heard speaking Catalan or dancing the traditional Sardana in the street. Wandering around in my exploratory walks, I felt a sense of apprehension if I moved away from frequented areas. How would I account for my presence if challenged? I felt this so acutely the day I walked along the deserted sea front to look at the statue of Columbus that I turned back halfway. You took care to avoid possible trouble.

Life at Madame's was enlivened by the periodic visits of Manolo's two blind uncles and supporting aunts. They were senior figures in one of the national lotteries for the blind and came on visits to the Barcelona office, in which Manolo worked. There was some suggestion that they had been blinded in the Moroccan campaigns but I never dared ask. I gradually became comfortable with them and got used to having my face felt: 'Who have we here? Ah, don Alejandro!' On St Cecilia's Day I went with Manolo to the great gathering of the blind in the Sagrada Familia. They sat, row upon row, in the twilight gloom of the cathedral, eating bread and cheap chocolate, their chatter lost in the cavernous roof, the children running around. The scene was a painting by Velazquez and brought to mind Lazarillo and the blind beggar.

Atkinson wrote from time to time about his advancing plans for the expedition to Spitsbergen and I agreed to be back in the UK after Easter. I did not want to hitchhike back through France. In the romantic vision I had of my visit to Spain I would end it by working my passage home on a ship and, when Manolo announced his intention to visit his mother in Seville for Easter, I saw the way open up. From Seville I would continue to Gibraltar where, with my usual confidence, I felt sure that I would find a ship. I started saving up for the train fares.

We broke the journey in Madrid and stayed two or three days with Manolo's uncle and aunt. Manolo took me to the Prado and we strolled around in much the same general atmosphere as in Barcelona. In the apartment the radio was turned on throughout the day, in contrast to Barcelona where we rarely heard it. At the end of programmes came the invocation to patriotism in sepulchral tones: 'Fallen for the country! Present! Up with Spain! Long live Franco!' followed by Cara al Sol, the Falange anthem. The Sunday Mass was broadcast which eased the conscience of the stay-at-homes. How my mother would have approved.

On to Seville. Manolo's mother, a widow, lived in a dark apartment opening onto a shared inner courtyard. I was turned loose most of the time and went to see the sights, the Alcazar, the Torre del Oro, La Giralda and so forth, but what I most enjoyed was simply being in Seville, breathing in the fragrance of orange blossom and bringing to life the Seville of my reading. Here was Calle Sierpes, just as in Cervantes. In that very street, I sat and watched the Holy Week procession of heavy brocaded floats with swaying statues. La Virgen de la Macarena passed unsteadily by. The float was put down and sweating men poked their heads out under the drapery.

The time came to say goodbye and to make promises of everlasting communication, sadly as usual to be of limited duration. The train to La Linea was slow and uncomfortable. I was in third (or was it fourth?) class with slatted wooden seats and in the same compartment there was a group of seasonal workers, gypsies in my imagination, moving on. As time drifted by they drew me into conversation, difficult to follow, and offered food.

I checked out of Spain and walked along the long curve of the causeway to the Gibraltar border. Far from being welcomed as a returning prodigal I was asked just one question: 'How much money do you have?' A few pesetas. Without the means to support myself I could not be admitted, and the border guard suggested that I seek help from the British Consul in La Linea. I walked back along the causeway and explained my purpose to the Spanish border guard who, rather to my surprise, cancelled the exit stamp and let me back into Spain.

I loafed the night away and saw the Consul the following morning. He explained that he was only a Vice-Consul dealing with shipping matters and had no funds. All he could suggest was that the Consul in Seville might be able to help or, if that were impractical, to go back to Gibraltar when a different guard was on duty and claim to have £25. Returning to Seville was out of the question, so I exited Spain again and as I approached the Gibraltar border a voice rang out: 'Did you get any money?' It was pointless to pretend, and with no alternative I trudged back to the Spanish guard who, to my satisfaction, refused to re-admit me to Spain. I retraced my steps, walking along the causeway for the sixth time in two days.

I sat down outside the border gate and waited. After a while one of the guards, perhaps going off duty, passed a sandwich between the bars and a short time later more food was passed to me, more than I could eat, which I hid in my rucksack for fear of being thought unappreciative. Eventually, the stand-off came to an end. I surrendered my passport to an official and was driven to the Sailors' Mission. In that bare and cheerless establishment I found two Czechs, young men, who had been spotted as stowaways on a ship bound for Australia and put ashore in Gibraltar. They had been there for months waiting for a decision on their fate. I felt for them. Being stuck in Gibraltar with nothing to do and no money to spend, as I came to know even in my short stay, was soul destroying.

My fate was out of my hands. Despite this I did not abandon my plan which was still within the realms of possibility. Through the Sailors' Mission I made contact with Merchant Navy officers who were themselves waiting for a ship home, one of whom said that he would see what he could do to fix me up. However, there was no time for that and I was unceremoniously put aboard a troopship heading for Liverpool. Apart from eating there was nothing to do, and to relieve the tedium I spent much of the voyage playing Monopoly with children. Shortly before landing, a passenger asked if I would take 200 cigarettes ashore for him, promising that he would 'see me right'. I did so and in return he gave me a measly two shillings. At least it enabled me to take the tram to Auntie Alice's to say hello before hitchhiking back to Luton. That proved to be my last visit to the family in Liverpool.

Quién hubiese tal ventura! Who should have such fortune! These words, the opening words of a 15th century 'romance' or ballad, have run through my mind while writing and recalling the twists and turns of my Spanish adventure. Like the good Count Arnaldo out hunting, I chanced upon a wondrous experience.

Spitsbergen

After Iceland, Atkinson could not be satisfied with some mundane site for the independent fieldwork he had to do at the end of his second year. With typical overreach, he selected Greenland but soon found it a step too far and his attention turned to Spitsbergen. Reading up about Spitsbergen he came across the name of Lancelot Fleming, Bishop of Portsmouth and erstwhile Spitsbergen explorer, and wrote to him for information about getting to Spitsbergen. The Bishop's advice was to contact a former fellow explorer, Alexander Glen, who was 'in shipping'. Atkinson did so and learned from him of the regular movement of ships transporting coal to Norway during the summer months. Glenn thought we should be able to obtain passage on one of these ships.

On the basis of this optimistic assumption the expedition to Spitsbergen came into being. The site chosen by Atkinson for his fieldwork presented a further imponderable. It was at the northern end of Prince Charles Foreland, a fifty-four-mile long finger of rock lying off West Spitsbergen, the main island of the Svalbard archipelago, and some eighty miles beyond the principal settlement Longyearbyen. It captured the imagination. There, surely, was the place to be, alone on an uninhabited island 600 miles from the North Pole, amid rock and ice and snow. It fired the blood. We would get there somehow. I cut short my stay in Spain and returned, prosaically, to Luton to earn some money for my contribution to costs. Imperial College provided a grant of £60 and Atkinson expected his father to help.

The Labour Exchange sent me to a honey bottling plant where I presented myself to Mr Gulliver, the foreman. The little factory had about ten employees under the charge of Mr Lewis, referred to behind his back as 'old Louie'. There were three labourers of whom I was one, a mechanic who operated the bottling machine, three women who handled the bottles and old Louie's secretary. It was a pleasing work family and I thoroughly enjoyed my six or seven weeks there, much of them spent mopping honey from the floor. There was one dramatic occasion when Mr Gulliver failed to close the drain of the machine which pumped the heated honey up to the bottling machine on the floor above. Old Louie burst into the blending room, where we were as usual mopping up, crying 'Gulliver has pumped 800 pounds of honey on the floor'. We found the bemused Gulliver stranded in the honey. We fetched shovels, scooped it up and put it back in the drum to be reheated and bottled.

I took on organising the expedition's food. We clearly needed more and better than we had had in Iceland and I worked out a simple diet of high calorific value, drawing guidance on quantities and relative proportions of protein, fat, and sugar from the chapter on food in the Royal Geographic Society's Hints to Travellers Part 2. This splendid handbook contained a wealth of information about sledges and dog harnesses and dog training drawn from the journals of polar expeditions, but was not limited to polar travel. It also advised how to guard against the depredations of insects in Africa, which put me off all thoughts of a career in the Colonial Service.

Pemmican: the iconic food of the great polar expeditions. I was determined that we should have it. It is basically a solid mixture of meat fibre and fat which, when heated with water, makes an unappealing greasy drink with sludge. I wrote to Bovril, enquiring whether they still made pemmican and, if so, would they be so kind as to provide us with free supplies. This they did, and so did all the manufacturers I propositioned: the Co-op for butter and oats, Peak Freen and Carr for biscuits, Cadbury and Fry for chocolate, all to be delivered to Atkinson's father's shop where he made wooden boxes for their transport and stencilled them with the letters PCFE, Prince Charles Foreland Expedition.

We needed a tent that could be put up easily by one man in bad conditions and, not finding one in the shops, had one made to my design. In this, the stitched-in groundsheet was extended to form a wide valance on which rocks could be placed to weight the tent down, but the new feature of the design was the use of jointed aluminium poles in sleeves on the outside of the tent which, when slotted into eyelet holes in the groundsheet, would put the tent up in one operation. The tent had a sleeve entrance, the groundsheet inside a retractable flap for cooking and a fore-and-aft guy to provide tension.

What about climbing gear, medical supplies, and communications? With the sublime confidence of youth we decided to do without them. A rope would not be needed as we would avoid doing any climbing requiring one. Confronted by the range of items required in a medicine chest, we decided to restrict ourselves to a bottle of iodine which we had found effective in Iceland for treating burst blisters, a packet of Elastoplast and a bottle of aspirins. As for communications, there were ex-Army kits to be had but we could not operate them. We would have to rely on waving.

Anticipating that the flat expanse of the north of the island would be snow-covered we bought two pairs of skis from an Army surplus store. We took no account of the fact that we had never skied, assuming that the technique required to shuffle across snow would not be hard to acquire. There were however consequences: the ski bindings required boots with square toes which, as they had also to be suitable for all purposes, we had to have made. In the event, we tried the skis only once and found them not only unnecessary but a burden, which left us with odd-looking square-toed boots to no useful purpose.

The plan was that I should go as advance party to Oslo to see about our passage to Spitsbergen. As the date for departure approached, I had to do something about retrieving my passport which had been impounded in Gibraltar when I was repatriated as a DBS. I went to London to see the Crown Agents, the agents for the Colonies, and was told that I would get my passport back when I paid the cost of my repatriation and stay in Gibraltar. The official answered my question about the location of my passport obliquely, allowing me to think that it might still be in Gibraltar. Alarmed by this, I hastened back to London with the sum required. The official took the passport from a drawer in his desk and handed it over with a bleak smile.

One morning in June I took the train to Newcastle, carrying one of the boxes. Leaving the box in left luggage, I made my way to Sunderland to find a ship bound for Oslo. Having located one, I simply went on board and knocked on the cabin door. I explained that I was the advance party of a scientific expedition to Spitsbergen and asked if they would be good enough to take me to Oslo where I had to report to the Norwegian Polar Research Institute. I said nothing about paying. Whether they believed me or admired my chutzpah, they invited me on board. After collecting my box from the station, I was installed in a four-berth cabin and fed and watered.

As we ploughed across the North Sea in the night we sat around drinking in the saloon. Very inexperienced about alcohol, I drank far too much and, after gulping gin from the bottle and declaring that it tasted like water, I passed out. Put to bed, I came to while vomiting and, seeing nothing better to do, transferred to one of the other berths in the cabin where I also vomited. Moving on, I hoped it would be third time lucky but, alas, it was not to be and I got into the remaining bunk conscious that it was my last chance. In the morning, the steward took the clearing up in his stride and nothing was said about the disgraceful behaviour of their non-paying guest.

In Oslo, I booked myself into the youth hostel and, leaving behind the box, went straight to the Norsk Polarinstitutt which has oversight of expeditions to Spitsbergen. The person I saw was supportive of our plans and, with regard to transport, said that I should go to Store Norske, as the Norwegian Spitzbergen Coal Company was familiarly known, and talk to a Mr Somethingsen, his name forgotten. Mr Somethingsen, however had different ideas. He told me coldly that Store Norske did not own the ships, only chartered them, and that it was company policy not to carry passengers other than company staff. I pressed him on this, arguing that we had a serious purpose, and finally extracted from him that the only basis on which they would carry us was at the request of the ship owner. Pressing further, I got out of him the name of the ship owner, Hilmar Reksten, and grudgingly the information that he was currently in Oslo.

I set off to find Mr Reksten and, enquiring at the most prestigious hotel in Oslo, found that he was staying there. There was no reply from his room so I settled down opposite the lift to wait for him. Whenever I saw a man whose appearance and demeanour suggested that of a ship owner, I went up and asked. After many a failure, I suddenly found myself talking to Mr Reksten and hurriedly explained our purpose mentioning, as I drew to a close, that we had been in touch with Alexander Glen. It seemed a magic word. Mr Reksten stopped me in my tracks and simply said, 'Tell Mr Somethingsen that I said yes.' We shook hands and went our different ways, mine in triumph back to the unhappy Mr Somethingsen. 'Very well', he said, 'report to the Store Norske wharf at Harstad.' When I put out my hand to shake his on parting, he extended one finger.

I collected the box and took the train to Trondheim where a few days later I intercepted Atkinson travelling north on the coastal steamer. On arrival in Hatstad in the Lofoten Islands we reported to the Store Norske office as directed and, anxious not to miss the boat, set up camp on the wharf. Days later, we were at last on our way to Spitsbergen, some 600 miles beyond Norway. We stood on the prow of the ship as it got under way, revelling in the icy breath of the Arctic, satisfied and elated.

We docked at Longyearbyen, on old maps Longyear City, originally and at that time still essentially a mining company town with a scatter of buildings. Today, it is the Sharm el Sheikh of the north. You can fly there throughout the year, book your hotel and car in advance, peruse the menu of restaurants, go on a sightseeing cruise to the nine nature reserves, visit the World Seed Bank, attend university and even go there on Google Earth without leaving your chair.

On landing, we were rather surprised to be directed to the Governor's Residence and even more surprised to be warmly received by the Governor himself. In a daze we were shown to a bedroom and invited to re-join the Governor for refreshments. We sat long over our drinks, unable to judge when to withdraw. Continuous daylight is disorienting, time stretches and conventional markers such as mealtimes and bedtime are blurred. As the Governor was in an expansive mood we raised the ticklish question of our transport to Prince Charles Foreland. With a wave of his hand he said that his motor vessel, the Sysla, would take us.

The Governor seemed in no hurry so, after an exchange of meaningful glances, we made a start on the intelligence brief for visitors to Spitsbergen which Atkinson had been given at the Ministry of Defence, seemingly a standard arrangement. We had beforehand divided the questions between us and made notes which we had in our pockets. Relaying between the lounge and the lavatory to note down the Governor's answers and mug up the next question, we worked through the brief. Somewhat to our surprise and gratification, the Governor seemed not to tire from talking about the output from the Russian mines and such matters, as his guests in turn reopened their interrogation on return from the lavatory.

As we moved to a close, the Governor himself asked a question: would we be visiting the aeroplane as usual? It was indeed our intention. Concealment was in vain. The Governor had been taken through the MOD brief before, and he himself told us where to find the wreck of the German warplane which was stranded on a landing strip that proved too soft. Our simple task was to measure the distance between the ground and the axle of the wheels, evidently to determine the rate of sinking, information surely of no practical use.

The next day we set off on the final leg of the journey, a further seventy odd miles by sea, to a trapper's hut near the northern tip of Prince Charles Foreland. The Governor's yacht headed first along Isfjorden, on which Longyearbyen lies, to the open sea and then north up the sheltered Foreland Sound, giving us our first sight of the jagged mountain range and glaciers of the island. We caught a passing glimpse of the Devil's Thumb, a huge tower of rock abutting the main mountain mass and marked it down for climbing one day. We were put ashore and carted our heavy and awkward boxes over the shingle and up to the hut, relieved to be rid of them, particularly the coffin-like ski box over which Atkinson's father had laboured.

Having cleared away the stores, our first action was to race across the island and climb to the top of the highest mountain in our expedition area from which, like Cortez on Darien peak, we stood looking out over the ocean wide. It was deeply satisfying to be at last on our island, 2,000 miles from Luton with only sea and ice between us and the North Pole. We were free, free to do what we liked when and how we liked. Here we were, two nineteen-year-old lads, larking about, wearing the clothes we wore for rock climbing in Wales. I had on the child's coat with the sleeves torn off.

On return from this foray we set about installing ourselves in the hut. There were two rooms: an outer store-room and the insulated inner living room. We unpacked our stores in the first and lit the fire in the stove in the other. I prepared our first supper of pemmican hoosh: half a tin of pemmican, two ounces of oats to thicken, heated with water to form a thick soup, served with croutons of crumbled ship's biscuit, one pint each in an enamelled tin mug. It tasted like Bovril and we never tired of it. Our rations were more than adequate and it was puzzling after a while to have food fantasies such as we had experienced in Iceland. The explanation lay in our ever-lengthening workday in the continuous daylight which settled at around twenty hours absence, hut to hut. We were eating food for twenty-four hours in a thirty-six-hour day.

We got down to work. Atkinson's objective was the study of the junction of two rock series to demonstrate geological continuity with the mainland. In addition, in the absence of an adequate map, we were to make a detailed topographical map of the area on which to plot the dips and strikes of the geological survey. We thus made a plane-table traverse of about eleven square miles in which I became increasingly involved. Simple in concept, it nevertheless required close attention to detail and much toing and froing. Once the grid had been established I took on all the topographical detail, working with two barometers and the abney level. I thus advanced from fellow adventurer and bag carrier to assistant surveyor.

There are bird cliffs at the northern tip of the island where thousands upon thousands of sea birds nest on the narrow, often grassy, ledges between the bands of rock. Movement and noise were unceasing in the continuous daylight until, with the advent of September, the sun dipped lower each day beneath the horizon and the cries of the birds died away to an eerie silence in the gathering dusk. We watched Arctic foxes in search of prey negotiating the narrow ledges, jumping up and down between the different levels, and one day thought to do the same to make a quick descent from the ridge. What a mistake. After slithering down a few ledges we realised that we were committed. There was no going back. All we could do was to hold our nerve and press on.

We were on the island for eight weeks or so and were due to depart in mid-September. By this time in the lengthening nights the temperature dropped perceptibly and we had snow. We were picked up as scheduled and retraced our steps to Luton. Our only disappointment from this expedition was that there was little snow and no ice to feed our yearning for the romance of polar exploration. We vowed that we would return and extend our work to the south which would take us onto the glaciers and snowy peaks of the island.

Cambridge

October, 1950. At last I was on my way to Cambridge, Magdalene College, the fulfilment of an ambition dating back, as I have described, to the playground of St Winifred's elementary school. Also 'going up' was a fellow schoolmate Peter Townsend, who had done well in the scholarship examinations, winning an Exhibition. We did not talk much on the journey, each savouring the moment. I had left school without a place at Cambridge and had only got in through the back door but I was in, which was what mattered.

Mr Townsend senior, who had driven us to Cambridge, dropped me off at the entrance to the college. The bowler-hatted porter ticked my name off his list and I walked in a dream across the courtyards to the Tutor's room where I learned, to my disappointment, that I would be living out of college for the first year. Back down to earth, I made my way to a modest house ten-minutes' walk from the college and settled myself in the two rooms provided, a bedroom and sitting room. I went back into town, hunted for a gown which I self-consciously put on, and wandered around until time for dinner at college. Submerged again in wonder, I took a place at the long tables in the candle-lit hall and sat in silent contemplation.

The following day, I met up with the other Modern Languages freshmen in the study of Dr Ladborough, beaming and genial as I remembered him, to work out the supervision timetable. We were not many, maybe seven or eight, including the three grammar school boys of the college intake of seventy freshmen. It was my first encounter with an Etonian. I marvelled at his ease and self-confidence in negotiating a time for supervision which did not interfere with beagling. Dr Ladborough was enthusiastic: 'Good Lord, you must go beagling', he said, and was indeed enthusiastic about anything we wanted to do: were we sure that we wanted to do Modern Languages? We could switch to anything we liked, how about cybernetics? We grammar school boys, having timidly accepted our supervision times, sat silently through this enthusiastic demolition of the established order.

Also taking Spanish was Terrence Bagshaw from Firth Park Grammar School, Sheffield, an unabashed Yorkshireman, and we went together to meet our Spanish supervisor, Dr Ines MacDonald, a lady whose enthusiasms, like those of Dr Ladborough, seemed unbounded. We learned later that she had been in Spain during the Civil War and she would have been a formidable presence, her fruity voice ringing out at the barricades. In addition to supervision with her, there was an optional oral practice class which we attended. Bagshaw lost interest when the lady running it was unable to get a grip on his name, calling him Bagshand at the second class we attended and Bagshat at the third. I too dropped out. After my time in Spain I was full of Spanish and had already taken the oral examination, passing it with a distinction, which I record as my one stellar achievement.

At college, I was ambushed by a giant of a man. 'You are needed by the third boat' he announced 'to cox it'. It was clear that a 'rather not, if you don't mind' reply would be swept aside and I was tickled by the proposition. It would be something new to try but needless to say the novelty quickly wore off. The skills required to cox the third boat were few and easily acquired and, while streaming along with rhythmic surges of power on a fine day was very agreeable, coxing consisted mostly of sitting huddled in the stern barking 'in-out' in cold damp air. Once committed, there was no escape. I coxed the third boat in races and, in my second year, was promoted to the second boat. In the summer bumps race, I had to wear a special second boat blazer, too big for me and reeking of mothballs, brought out from the college wardrobe. It was traditional to throw the cox in the river after the race but perhaps the blazer, too precious to risk being spoiled, saved me, though in fact I rather looked forward to it as a fitting conclusion to my career as a cox.

I decided to take the examination for Part 1 Spanish at the end of the first year and that for French the following year. Bagshaw chose to do the same and we went to the weekly supervision together. One day, in the hope of enlivening the occasion and seeking the approbration of Dr MacDonald, Bagshaw proposed that the popular radio show 'Take It From Here' was in essence a picaresque story. Dr MacDonald was enraptured. 'Fascinating!' she cried and then, after revealing that she had never heard the show, 'Do go on, Terry'. This was not what Bagshaw expected. He got so hopelessly lost in describing the characters and antics of Mr Glum and the hapless Ron and Eth that the good doctor lost patience and put an end to his rambling with a final 'Fascinating'. I had my moments. At the end of one term, Dr MacDonald listed several Shakespeare plays as essential vacation reading. I heard her say 'Nebuchadnezzar' and queried it. 'Measure for Measure' she warbled, 'Foolish boy!'.

I threw myself into all things Spanish. I became an active member of the Spanish Society, joining its choir and appearing in the production of a play. I attended soirees in the rooms of Professor Trend, the grand old man of the faculty, to hear tales of his time in Spain. He claimed to have been for a while secretary to Manuel de Falla; 'Tell me JB, Manuel said to me one day, what shall be the subject of my next opera? An Englishman in Seville, I said.' We listened to the scratchings of his old records in reverent silence. Despite this devotion to my subject the examiners judged me only worth a 2:1.

Inured to under-performing in examinations, I swallowed my disappointment and devoted my attention to our forthcoming return to Spitsbergen. Atkinson had kept me informed about progress in planning for the second expedition, and once approval had been given I had approached the same companies as on the first expedition for our food supplies, which they provided again free of charge. He came to Cambridge and together we called on Sir James Wordie, Master of St John's College and elder statesman of British polar exploration. Wordie was the chief geologist of Shackleton's renowned 1914 expedition in which the Endurance was crushed in the ice, and took part in nine subsequent polar expeditions. By an extraordinary coincidence he had a Prince Charles Foreland connection. He was part of the survey team sent by the Scottish Spitsbergen Syndicate to the island in the 1920s to look for coal which they found but not in exploitable quantity. Wordie had nothing of moment to tell us and it was an occasion for reminiscence, nonetheless enjoyable for that and we parted with his blessing.

Return to Spitsbergen

The aim of the second expedition was to extend the geological and topographical survey from the area covered in the first visit to the remainder of the island. As before, it had financial support from Imperial College, and the Royal Geographical Society (RGS) contributed the Gino Watkin's award for 1951 of £40. We counted on Store Norske again providing transport.

As this expedition would involve glacier travel we needed a sledge and man-hauling equipment. Atkinson tracked down a seven-foot ex-RAF Nansen sledge and I went to the London shop of Benjamin Edgington's, tent and camping manufacturers, in search of man-harnesses. Surely an esoteric item, I was disappointed when the storeman in his brown coat, far from expressing surprise, merely asked how many I required. The man-harnesses themselves were also a disappointment, consisting of an open canvas band to go around the waist with eyelets to attach the sledge rope and shoulder straps, a simple and cheap contraption. Was this all Captain Scott had?

In a visionary move, Atkinson bought an ex-RAF inflatable dinghy to be used to paddle stores for the forward base on the glacier along the shore. Like many a bright idea it did not work out in practice and the dinghy joined our other cast-offs. The one extra we did need was a flysheet for the tent and we had one made. Though the tent kept the rain out, it could not breathe when the canvas was wet and condensation formed.

A few weeks before departure a letter came from the RGS containing astonishing news: we were to join a large Cambridge expedition on board HMS Cook, a Royal Navy survey ship, for passage to Longyearbyen. Manna from Heaven! We sent our thanks over the ether to the kind person at RGS who had thought of us. We boarded the ship at Gourock on the Clyde. As a survey vessel, HMS Cook had a large complement of specialist officers who were very agreeable company. We had lunch with the Captain in his cabin and received every courtesy except from the leader of the Cambridge party, a seasoned academic, who could not take us, or rather me, a student of languages, seriously.

We left the ship at Longyearbyen and made our way to the Governor's residence, where he once again gave us his full support and arranged for the Sysla to take us to the island. We were put ashore at the same hut as the previous year. No larking about this time. Extending the survey to the rest of the island was an ambitious undertaking and we had a huge task before us. We got straight to work and in the two months that followed marched to and fro carrying stores, setting up the camps and climbing mountains, chipping away at rocks and making survey observations.

Combining pleasure with business, we reached the summit of every peak in the central and southern range, climbing to 2,000-3,500 feet from sea-level. On one descent we saw the opportunity to glissade down a snow slope which we could see ran out all the way to the bottom. It was not too steep and the snow was wet and heavy. We began jumping and sliding down the small avalanches we created, first standing then sitting, rolling from side to side to remain on top. It was good fun until I found myself in a groove in the underlying ice going ever faster driven by the snow piling up behind me. As the groove became deeper I was in my own uncontrollable Cresta Run.

Unable to brake I careered down as the ice walls rose around me, hoping that the groove was not blocked. At the bottom I was spewed out with my avalanche onto the mud, soaked to the skin.

It was only towards the end of the expedition when, in late August, we had to set up by sledge a camp on the glacier, that we came at last within reach of our dream of polar travel. However it proved to be a nightmare. To start with, the surface was not snow but ice on which the sledge runners had no purchase. Secondly, our direction of travel lay across the glacier which sloped down to the sea so that the sledge slid sideways. Atkinson pulled the sledge whilst I, with shoulder to the side of the sledge, held it to its course but the sledge, top heavy, kept tipping over and the effort of righting was so great that we split the load and made two journeys.

Camping on the ice was no fun. As it was summer the glacier was wet and, when it rained, ran with water which flowed over the flaps of the groundsheet and seeped into the tent. The rain was remorseless. Everything in the tent was wet. We lay in our wet sleeping bags on our air-bed islands taking turns to hold the oats on our chest to keep them dry. At times, bored and cramped, we would get up and go for a walk to stretch our legs, and on return wring out our clothes and sleeping bags and get back in them. There seemed no end to the rain.

However the rain did stop, and it was now or never for the attempt on the Devil's Thumb, the 2,700 ft tower of rock buttressing the mountain. Its chisel-shaped summit, standing clear of the mountain mass, rises 2000 ft from the glacier, sheer on one side but at a more inviting angle on the other. Later, I wrote an article describing the ascent for the Cambridge University Mountain Club journal. With the usual hyperbole of climbing accounts, it makes the ascent seem much harder technically than it could possibly have been as we were climbing without ropes and in our heavy square-toed boots. Nonetheless the climb, a sustained steep scramble with hard-to-reverse passages on cold wet rock, was a risky undertaking. There was no way back, we were committed and had to pin our hopes on there being an alternative way down. After building a cairn to mark our ascent, we climbed back down the easier-angled summit ridge and found to our great relief that it was possible to traverse from the col onto the snow of the main mountain mass and so down, finding a way though the bergschrunds, the crevasses between mountain and ice. My article concludes:

> '... as we walked over the ice in a heavy downpour, we cared not for our wet, tired and aching bodies: we had done it! Twenty exciting hours had seen the fulfilling of our ambition, we basked in the afterglow of satisfaction... but the thought of sleeping bag and pemmican hoosh was both pleasant and alluring.'

Hurrah for the pemmican! After this epic we spent further days on the ice, hampered by the continuing bad weather, then it was back to the hut to pack up. We were picked up by the Store Norske cutter, the Polar Kull, on its way to the mining operation at Ny Ålesund, further north on the mainland. There we did the tourist thing and had our passports stamped and dated at the self-proclaimed Most Northerly Post Office in the world.

In his note on the expedition for the Polar Record, Atkinson states that in our sixty-day journey we had covered 700 miles and a separate reference in the Record describes the expedition as a 'tour de force'. We were certainly conscious of having pulled off a monumental task and left the island well satisfied with ourselves. As in the previous year, we vowed to return and even speculated about over-wintering.

On return to Longyearbyen, we found a Birmingham University party awaiting passage to Tromso to rejoin the boat they had chartered for their expedition, which had been refused permission to proceed by the Norwegian authorities because it was not strengthened for ice. We got on well with the Birmingham party and, when we reached Tromso, they invited us to join them for the return voyage to Liverpool, at £15 apiece. First HMS Cook, then this. Who should have such fortune!

The Miss Mabel was a 114 ft motor launch converted from wartime service as a high-speed craft for clandestine sea journeys by replacing its three 2000 hp petrol engines with 100 hp diesel engines. Its owner and skipper was a retired Lieutenant RN and the crew consisted of a director of Ferranti who had come along for the trip, and an adventure-seeking young man who had offered his services from the dockside in Liverpool. Stuck in Tromso with nothing to do until the return of the expedition party, the crew had spent their time doing maintenance work, rubbing down and re-varnishing the woodwork. They tried but failed to repair the centre engine which had given out during the journey north.

We piled onboard and were soon off down the Norwegian coast heading for Kristiansand to refuel for the final stage to Liverpool. A couple of days later, on the look-out for Kristiansand, when nothing came into view, not even the coast, and it became evident that a navigational error had occurred, traceable to the faulty repositioning of the compass taken down in the maintenance work in Tromso. In due course, refuelled and the compass put in order, we set off back across the North Sea, making for Inverness and the Caledonian Canal.

In the middle of the North Sea a further mishap occurred: the boat started to go round in circles. It transpired that all three blades of one of the two remaining propellers had sheared off. We were now reduced to one engine and, changing course, we headed very slowly to Lerwick in Shetland. There, the boat was beached on a hard and the propeller from the defunct centre engine was switched to the damaged engine. We set off again for Inverness, thence along the Caledonian Canal into the Irish Sea and, finally, Liverpool and the end of a highly satisfying journey.

Cambridge – the remaining years

On walking into the college on my return I bumped into my tutor: 'Oh hallo' he said, 'just back from Greenland?' I learned that I was to live, not in the ancient part of the college as I had hoped, but in Mallory Court across the road. I lapsed into feckless student behaviour. I was disenchanted with French. I attended only one lecture and, finding it crowded and boring when audible, never went again. I coxed, took up squash, appeared in another Spanish play, courted my future wife, an undergraduate at Newnham College, and in the evenings played poker for harmless stakes. I banked on passing the end-of-year examination with what I had learned for Higher School Certificate plus a little polish from supervisions. Dr Ladborough, after coasting through our first year when we were concentrating on Spanish, was now in full play. Part of the weekly session was spent going over the translations set by him which usually contained some syntax or vocabulary difficulty chosen for its amusement potential. Set to translate 'motes of dust dancing in the sunlight,' the words chosen by my fellow supervisee came out in retranslation as 'little pieces of excrement' to the hilarity of all, especially of Dr Ladborough who rocked to and fro holding his sides.

I got a 2:2 in the examination which was more than I deserved. I was ashamed of the neglect of my studies and decided that an injection of something new and requiring effort was called for in my final year. I proposed to Peter Townsend that we take the Italian Renaissance paper and, in Spanish, I took on the Conquest of Latin America paper. In consequence, I was able to jettison two literature papers which examination after examination showed were my weakness.

However, was it a reckless move? The two new subjects were huge, and for the Renaissance paper we needed to be at ease with Italian. I looked around for a summer course and found one at the University for Foreigners in Perugia which ran an introductory course in September. I booked our places and applied to the Bedfordshire Education Authority, the provider of my maintenance grant, for a supplementary award to which, against expectation, they agreed.

To raise money for the visit to Italy, I applied to the Labour Exchange in Luton for a job and was sent to Laporte Chemicals to fill a vacancy in the Stores Department. Its staff consisted of the manager approaching retirement, two counter hands and me, whose undemanding job it was to keep an eye on the stock in the bins and alert the manager to shortages. Of the two counter hands, one was a tall ex-Guardsman with bad teeth and the other, his silent shadow, who listened with rapt attention to the tales of misbehaviour and sexual antics in the barracks. Laporte's was not a salubrious place in which to work. There were factory hands whose skins were bluish white from contact with chemicals used to make brilliant white paint and the air had an acrid taste due to the condensation of sulphuric acid fumes. You got used to it, however.

The manager went off on his summer holidays without leaving any instructions. I tentatively began reordering and progressively took charge of his desk, unchallenged by the two storemen. Halfway through August I gave notice of my departure. A man in a suit came across from the offices to say how pleased they were with my work and wanted me to stay on and take over the manager's job when he retired.

We planned to hitch-hike to Italy but gave ourselves a flying start by taking the train to Paris. We stayed overnight in the cavernous gloom of Stade Malakoff, a disused stadium, watching latecomers pick their way like grave robbers through the maze of mattresses on the floor. We struggled as far as Fontainebleau the next day and on the following waited in vain at the roadside. Eventually, a lorry stopped, heading for Orange, a distance of some 400 miles, a fantastic lift but there was a condition: the driver wanted payment, not a large sum. We looked at each other and climbed into the cab. From Orange we got a further lift late in the day to Avignon. The night was warm and windless. I proposed that we should sleep à la belle étoile and so we did, wrapped in discarded newspapers, on heathland looking out over the river and its truncated bridge.

It took us the whole following day of short lifts to cover the 150 miles to the Riviera and the border with Italy. We crossed it on foot and from nearby Ventimiglia we were lucky to pick up a lift to Florence despite the late hour. Talking all the time, the Italian driver entertained us with feats of driving, taking hairpin bends in four-wheel drift, which had us shuttling from side to side in the back seat. No safety belts in those days. What a driver, though, he drove the 250 miles without stopping and put us down in Florence late at night outside a small hotel.

The hotel was close to the central square and turning into it the following morning we beheld a breathtaking sight. The Cathedral reared up in improbable black and white layers and, facing it, stood Michelangelo's David with his long arms and outstretched hand, so natural as to invite touch. In a dream, we wandered around eating croquetas from a rough grey paper cone. A morning in Florence, unforgettable.

We worked through the list of what we wanted to see in Florence, unhampered by the crowds of today. In succeeding days we hitched to Arezzo to see the Piero della Francesca mural, then to Assisi for the Giotto murals and finally, journey's end, to Perugia. We were accommodated in the student quarters and ate in the refectory with others attending courses. The teachers taught by the direct method which never works very well with me. To make sense of the soup of vowels and indistinct consonants I hear, I need to see it written down. However, what was being taught with histrionic gestures and facial contortions was mostly already known by us and indeed the course as a whole added little in knowledge, but much in confidence in using what we knew.

Attending the same course were Karen Bliss, the daughter of Sir Arthur, Master of the Queen's Music, and John Attenborough, younger brother of the famous Richard, and yet to be famous David. At the end of the course we headed for Rome, Karen by train and the three of us hitch-hiking. We were dropped off near the Pantheon and were directed by a passer-by to 'somewhere cheap to stay'. It was certainly cheap: a Church-run hostel for the indigent with mattresses on the floor, a few lire a night. We ate in a nearby restaurant with pay-at-the-door meals and tickets of different colours for each of the three courses. By arrangement, we met up with Karen and she brought to the meeting the Canadian studying opera, to whom she had an introduction. He was companionable, knew his way about Rome and seemed to have plenty of money. He took us in hand and for three days drove us in his big American car to whatever we wanted to see. At the end of each morning tour he gave us all lunch, not of the three ticket variety but, memorably, on our last day at a restaurant at the foot of the Spanish Steps. Who should have such fortune!

We took the train home and returned to Cambridge a few days later for our third and final year. My supervisor for the Latin America paper was a young academic who had yet to acquire the airs and graces of the Cambridge don. Not long since a student himself, he understood the burden of ignorance and the tone of the supervisions was brotherly. However, he did not disguise the amount of learning to be done and there were times, bogged down with detail and unmemorable names, I even yearned for Baudelaire.

Our supervisor for the Renaissance paper was Dr Joyce Reynolds, Dante scholar and friend and biographer of Dorothy L Sayers.

Surprisingly, we were the only two taking the paper. The two-hour sessions started at the unfriendly hour of nine o'clock and, sitting across from her at a desk in the lecture room, there was no hiding place. In the non-stop discursive flow of information it was all we could do to look attentive, let alone take notes. One afternoon, she took us in her car to visit a colleague to see his not very compelling collection of Commedia dell'Arte memorabilia. His cottage, old and dark, was so crammed with exhibits that there seemed to be no living space, and I wondered at the consuming passion that drove him.

We laboured through our last year. The academic life which had once seemed so attractive was now a burden. We longed to be up and away into the real world. The final examinations came along, their promise of release overlain by anxiety and regret for time frittered away. Apart from the two new papers, the examination included old standby subjects such as the French Romantic Poets for the last time. I was relieved to pass with a 2:2, concluding that the examiners in the new papers must have been the supervisors themselves concerned for their charges. What did it matter anymore? I was at last free from captivity. I packed my bags and left for Spitsbergen.

The final expedition

The best part of two years had elapsed since the second expedition and during this time Atkinson and I went our separate ways. We did not seek each other's company and on the few occasions we met we were, to begin with, rather awkward with each other. We were each making our own way in life and would have drifted apart but were held together by the promise made of a third expedition. I clung to it as an article of faith but my heart did not leap at the prospect of returning to Spitsbergen again for more of the same. I had got all I wanted out of Spitsbergen and if the expedition had been called off I would have shed few tears.

For Atkinson it was a different matter. He was now working on his doctoral thesis and at the beginning of 1953 he put forward plans for the third expedition. In a new departure, he proposed that we should acquire a boat to be able to carry out a two-phase programme, firstly to move quickly between sites on the island requiring follow-up work and secondly, to cross to an area on the main island to study a complementary rock series. The ambitious proposal found favour with London University and the RGS and funds were provided, including a grant from the Linnaeus Society, to cover the overall cost estimated to be £260. My college provided a modest £15. Multiplication by ten gives a rough idea of the value of these sums in today's money.

It was taken for granted that I would play my customary role. It was business as usual. I put aside my hesitations and formed a rosy vision of scudding about the island by boat and of setting foot in the splendidly named King Haakon VII Land, the site of the proposed survey on the main island. Atkinson arranged to buy the boat of a departing miner and approached Seagull Motors for the loan of not one but two outboard engines, one of 3.5hp and the other of 1hp to propel the kayak he had bought. He did not consult me about the acquisition of the kayak for which there was demonstrably no need. Did he see it as essential to the image of the expedition? Had he been reading up Greenland expeditions?

My contribution, as before, was to organise the food, which I did, pounding away on a portable typewriter in my college room. The suppliers responded generously yet again and Mr Atkinson senior dusted off the old PCFE crates. 1953 was the Everest year and, having read somewhere that a well-known manufacturer was providing knitwear for the expedition, I cheekily wrote asking for any socks that might be surplus. A large cardboard box arrived from which, when eventually opened in Spitsbergen, poured forth a dazzling cascade of red, yellow, emerald green and sky blue, a cornucopia of socks in small, medium, and large, six pairs of each, in all seventy-two pairs of socks. I had omitted to mention that we were a two-man party.

To provide extra time for the two-part programme, we set off at the beginning of June. As we steamed up the Norwegian coast we sat in the sun listening to the news of the conquest of Everest, the Coronation and much euphoric talk of a new Elizabethan age. On reaching Longyearbyen, by courtesy once more of Store Norske, we sought out the boat Atkinson had bought. To our eyes, the sleek carvel-built boat some eighteen feet long seemed just what was required and we swelled with pride of ownership.

After the now familiar preliminaries at the Governor's Residence, our new prize possession was loaded onto the deck of the Sysla and we were on our way back to Prince Charles Foreland. The Sound was open though some ice still clung to the shore on which seals basked. The crew ferried our possessions ashore, leaving the boat at the water's edge for us to haul up above the high tide line. We then discovered how heavy it was to handle. We had to dig a channel in the deep snow above the tide-line and it took us an ominous amount of effort to drag it. Our base this time was the superior hut built by the Scottish Spitsbergen Syndicate in the 1920s, some twenty miles to the south of our previous hut and better located for our purposes.

We were keen to try out our prize possession and hauled it down to the water's edge. As the beach was shallow and the boat deep in draught it did not readily float clear, and we had to wade out still dragging the boat. When the water was up to our knees, we thought better of it and waded back to the shore where we took all our clothes off and, throwing them in the boat, stepped back into the icy water. At waist deep and jabbering with cold we clambered on board and I fumbled with the engine. The practice of wading out became routine, even wading out deeper until the feet lifted off the bottom in order to get the boat as far offshore as possible, though thenceforth we kept our clothes on, preferring it to the shock of the cold water. Once underway we took them off, wrung them out, put them back on and shivered.

The motor would not start. I tried it this way and then that, twenty, thirty, forty pulls of the starter cord. When all seemed lost, the motor suddenly burst into life and the boat began to move. It did not go as fast as I imagined or hoped it would, it seemed no more than a fast walking pace. The vision of scudding about the island with a foamy wake was already a faded dream.

But wait, there was still the kayak. One site for reinvestigation lay three or four miles away on the long curve of the coast. The sky was blue, the sea was calm: it was perfect for a trial run across the bay. I fashioned a wooden strut, jammed in place amidships, to which the 1hp engine could be clamped. We got afloat with no more than wet feet and paddled clear. The motor fired at once and we set off across the millpond, again slower than hoped but it was effortless, a joyride. Hours later, however, when it was time to return, the sky was grey and the sea ruffled by a fresh wind. Halfway across the bay the motor, close to the water level, began to splutter and was finally swamped by the rising sea. We now had to paddle and as we neared the shore the waves, growing ever larger, sloshed over the canvas and into the open cockpit. With 200 yards to go Atkinson, who was in front of me, stopped paddling. Consternation! This was no time for exhaustion. I shouted at him, pushed and prodded him and finally, hitting him as hard as I could with the paddle, I got him going again. There would be no more kayak trips.

Atkinson's unaccountable behaviour was perhaps a sign of things to come, for some weeks later his right knee stiffened up which he recognised as a recurrence of the osteomyelitis contracted during his schooldays. Back then, he had undergone surgery as antibiotics which control if not cure the infection were yet to come into general use. Our iodine and sticking plasters were of no use: penicillin was what he needed. Plunged in gloom, Atkinson retreated into himself and took to his bed.

Providentially we had the boat. I felt confident enough to undertake the crossing to Longyearbyen as we had used the boat a few times and Atkinson, aloof as captain of the ship, had left all the handling to me. When the sea was calm enough I jerked the boat down inch by inch and, leaving it half in the water, filled the tank and loaded up before fetching Atkinson who hobbled down, sleeping bag round his shoulders. He lay, hardly moving, for the whole journey of some sixty miles, first across the Sound then south to the mouth of Isafjord and along it to Longyearbyen.

We were soon in the ocean swell, sailing across the westerly wind. To reduce roll I had to bear up into the wind as each wave approached, then bear away down its back to hold the course. We zigzagged thus, rising and falling, every now and then refreshed by spray, before at last turning east into the fjord and into quieter waters. The sun came out, our clothes dried and sparkled with salt. The boat chugged along.

In the warmth it was hard to keep awake but one worry remained: would the fuel last out? At a guess, the crossing took ten hours, maybe more, maybe less, as we had no accurate measure of time. I had no watch and Atkinson did not wear his; we relied on the position of the sun or other indicators which was sufficient for our purposes.

We stayed at Longyearbyen for a week or so, which gave time to do something about the refuelling problem. During the journey I had had to refuel crouching over the stern, pouring fuel from the heavy jerry-can in the bucking and rolling boat, at risk of being tossed overboard. Furthermore, to avoid going round in circles whilst doing this, I had to turn off the motor with no certainty that it would start again. What was needed was a method of refuelling safely without shutting down the engine, and it took no great brain to see that a nozzle welded to both jerry-can and fuel tank plus a length of flexible connecting hose would do the trick. I took my proposed solution to the Radio Station workshop and the work was soon done.

It did not occur to me to ask the workshop to look into the starting difficulty which haunted all our journeys, as I regarded it as a manufacturer's fault since the motor had gone straight into use from the box and had never been tampered with. Seagull Motors, when the engine was returned to them, found the needle of the carburettor float to be out of alignment, implying that this was our doing. It was not but by then it no longer mattered.

After his time in the clinic Atkinson emerged, apparently as fit as a fiddle such was the effectiveness of penicillin, and we got a lift back to the island to avoid repeating the journey. The whole episode had taken some three weeks and there was now not enough time for phase two, the visit to King Haakon VII Land. There remained, however, the unfinished work of phase one, namely visiting sites on the west coast of Prince Charles Foreland, and on a fine day we set off half-way round the island, some sixty miles, to the first site to be revisited. Refuelling was a dream and the engine popped and gurgled without interruption. This was more like it.

When it was time to move on to the next site, the sea had settled after bad weather into a long, slow, deep swell which looked manageable provided we could get offshore which, in the large crashing waves, was questionable. We watched the waves and made our move. While I tackled the engine, Atkinson, poling with an oar, fought the incoming wave. We got away at the cost of the blade of the oar.

Riding the swell was exhilarating. The boat seemed motionless as it effortlessly mounted the wave, the water appearing to flow backwards beneath the hull. Then, toppling over the crest with a burst from the engine as the propeller broke the surface, the boat raced down into the trough where it seemed to stop in the face of next wave. Over and over again. Here and there white waves were breaking and, even as I hoped we would not be caught in one, the boat tilted sharply forward. Glancing over my shoulder I saw a mountain of water bearing down on us. It picked us up and tossed us into a turmoil of foam and then, just as suddenly, all became still and silent. The engine was dead, the boat adrift, full of water, rising and falling. My first thought was to throw overboard the box of rock specimens but we were still afloat. What if the engine would not start ? However, the Gods smiled, it fired into life and we scurried away into deeper waters, baling with empty pemmican tins.

It was a sobering experience. We were lucky not to have capsized. We were half a mile offshore in the cold waters of the Arctic Ocean and if we had been thrown overboard there would have been no rescue. We looked at each other and, without a word, abandoned the programme and headed back to base round the northern tip of the island, a journey of sixty miles and more given the sea room we had been obliged to take. Many hours later we hauled up the boat which had come to dominate our lives, taking up so much time and effort, the engine a constant worry. Deemed essential for the expedition, paradoxically the only essential use made of the boat was to take Atkinson to hospital.

All things considered, we had relatively little to show for our endeavours. The loss of phase two, around which the expedition was planned, was a particular disappointment to Atkinson as it denied him the opportunity to put the finishing touch to his work. In our remaining time on Prince Charles Foreland he studied his notes and I set about packing up. I made a drawing of the interior of the hut before dismantling the disarray in which we lived.

We had one last adventure on the journey home. Unexpectedly, we put in at the North Cape and at anchor nearby were two or three British trawlers. We saw the opportunity to avoid the long journey down the coast and, in our usual winning way, it was not long before we were on board one of the trawlers and under way, pitching and tossing decks awash, in the towering waves of the North Atlantic.

We spent most of our time on the bridge where the crew gathered to talk and listen to the ceaseless radio chatter between ships and shore. There was no apparent pecking order as the skipper dressed like the rest of the crew and indeed, as we learned, skippers could very well end up back in the crew if they did not have the knack of finding fish. The actual fishing part of each trip, between the journeys to and from the fishing grounds, was a dangerous round-the-clock operation in all conditions but now the crew were at ease on the way home for a short break before setting off to do it again. A hard life. We kept silent about our own adventures on the high sea.

There was one mess for all, a rather cramped saloon with a table taking up most of the floor space and, above the surrounding bench seat, a double tier of bunks lined the walls like stacked coffins. Slide the hatch back and choose any unoccupied one. There did not seem to be any undressing or washing, to which we were well accustomed. We ate fish and more fish. As we neared Hull the radio chatter fell away, the trawlers avoiding indication of their position as they jockeyed for the best time of arrival at the market. We docked and the crew sprang into life to be away for their brief shore leave. For us, our Spitsbergen travels were over.

After Spitsbergen

Back at home, my parents produced cuttings of three newspaper articles about the expedition which had appeared in the London Evening News. Atkinson told me before we set off that he had sold four articles to the press to raise money but he did not elaborate and never subsequently mentioned them. At the time, I assumed that they would be published on return, as on previous occasions, but here in my hand were the first three articles, rich in sensation and fantasy, presented as dispatches from the front line. How had Atkinson and the journalist contrived this illusion given that we had no communications?

It was of course a hoax. The articles were based on events, experiences, and photographs from the first two expeditions and were released during our absence in June, August, and the third in September, when we were on our way home in the trawler. This left the fourth article to be written after return and published while the expedition, according to the first article, was still in the field.

The real-time illusion was bolstered by the inclusion in the articles of two events which occurred during the expedition, neither of which Atkinson or the journalist could have foreseen when they made their arrangements. The first event was the avalanche which struck Longyearbyen in mid-June by which time we were already on Prince Charles Foreland. It was reported in the international press and picked up by the journalist who made it the lead story of the second article under the banner headline 'Avalanche!'. In the spirit of the hoax the journalist described our imaginary role in the clear-up, concluding with the words 'we have done what we can to help; now at long last we are on our way'.

The second event was Atkinson's knee problem which was presented in the third article as an injury caused by a dramatic rockfall followed by heroic self-rescue. The story was clearly written by Atkinson in the clinic and sent by post to the journalist. In the high days of our friendship Atkinson would have drawn me into this hoax, which was just the sort of trick we delighted in. The decision to keep it to himself perhaps reflected the change in our relationship or was some double-think of his part, but there was no point in speculating. I decided to let it go and say nothing, preferring not to enter another maze of deception.

It was back to the drawing board for me as I had to finish the map. Tidying up contours was straightforward but drawing the features of the flat southern area from air photographs taken at an oblique angle was mentally exhausting and could only be done with some degree of accuracy using specialised equipment. I seized on any excuse not to work on the map; I had my job and spent weekends visiting my wife-to-be in Cambridge. Atkinson justifiably complained and I was conscious of letting him down, but the more he nagged the more I resented his goading.

Matters came to a head when Atkinson demanded that I hand over the map. I took it to London and our meeting in his flat quickly collapsed into mutual recrimination. Atkinson stormed off with the map to his bedroom leaving his future wife, whom I knew well from my schooldays, to pacify us both. I was not to be appeased. I repeatedly demanded my drawing of the hut and when Atkinson at last surrendered it, I stormed out of the house with it. It was a sorry end to our relationship but it had run its course and that night in London

I broke free. I never saw or spoke with him again. Months later, a copy of the finished map arrived by post without an accompanying letter. I took it as acknowledgement of my contribution but I did not use the opportunity to write back and salvage the relationship.

In revisiting the whole Spitsbergen story, I have thought a lot about my relationship with Atkinson from early infatuation, comradeship, and the drift to eventual disillusion. I often wondered what became of him. When in later years I found myself in the company of oilmen I asked after him: none had never heard of him save one who said, 'Ah, the Spitsbergen stratigrapher'.

Some traces exist of our expeditions. Atkinson's PhD thesis is on-line, as are references to the expeditions in the official Polar Record, but there is nothing in the RGS archive. All that remains to me are copies of some of Atkinson's letters to the RGS, the map, the drawing of the hut and a clutch of photographs. In the hope of recovering expedition papers, especially the logbooks which I assiduously kept on all three expeditions, my daughter tracked down and contacted Atkinson's daughter in the United States, who searched the family papers for the logbooks but found only a few papers and photographs.

Atkinson's daughter, with whom we have formed a familial bond, talked freely about her father. She is under no illusions about him and readily recognised the man I knew. She described her disrupted childhood with her wayward father who careered from one job to another, moving from place to place, coming and going without warning. Despite this she always felt loved. He told wondrous stories and thought up exciting, even scary, adventures. She recalled his hippy phase into which the whole family was drawn. It was no half-measure: characteristically, her father immersed himself totally in the culture including going to India. His restlessness put the marriage under repeated strain and it finally broke up when he left to remarry.

Spitsbergen for the family meant forever packing and unpacking the old Spitsbergen tent and the kayak which her father could not let go of. From time to time he would reminisce about 'Mac', my school nickname, describing me as 'jovial' or 'the cleverest man I ever knew' or an 'ingenious fellow'. He regretted our break-up and acknowledged his part in it. Getting it wrong in his relationships was usual: he was able to make friends with people of interest to him but he could not keep them. The sad effect of this was that the family had no real friends at the end of his life. He died in 1997 at the age of 65.

Atkinson's daughter said that her father could always find or create work. After college he worked in Angola and then at times for Shell. He had two academic appointments, the second a professorship at Harvard which he lost by falling out with the faculty over his teaching methods. He worked in Tibet on a huge geothermal project and successfully applied to NASA for a place on the space training programme but failed the medical because of the osteomyelitis which dogged him throughout his life.

The picture the Atkinsons' daughter paints of her father's journey through life is that of a man in search of himself, never finding satisfaction and rest, driven constantly by the spirit of adventure as the forlorn application to NASA shows. It was simpler in our youthful years yet we still fell out, as we were bound to, but nothing diminishes the delight we found together in those early adventures in the mountains, in Iceland and in Spitsbergen, and for that I am in his debt.

Rothschilds

As the end of my third year at Cambridge grew ever closer, the prospect of having to go out into the real world loomed large and my thoughts turned towards my future employment. I had no idea what I wanted to do except to use my languages and not end up behind a desk. However, with the third Spitsbergen expedition before me, I decided that there was nothing to be done until I got back. I would surely find something then, after all jobs were many and graduates few in those days.

Despite having put my future firmly out of my mind, it would not leave my thoughts. What about the Colonial Service? There were a couple of probationers in college learning about Native Law and everything needed to govern the Empire, tall silent men with square jaws and an air of impending self-sacrifice. The prospect of a further year at Cambridge was not unattractive, but what I had read in the RGS Hints to Travellers about insect life in Africa was off-putting. In any case, I could not see myself sitting in a forest clearance dispensing justice.

The question of my future employment nagged away and eventually I gave in and went to see the Cambridge University Appointments Board, if only to stake my claim for the future. A few days later, to my surprise, I received instructions to present myself for interview with a City firm on the very eve of departure to Spitsbergen. It could not have been more ill-timed, but I thought it better to obey. I reported to the company offices in my college blazer and was received by the Chairman who was disconcerted by my appearance. He could not, he said, now take me to lunch at his club as he had intended and we would have to make do with a restaurant. At the restaurant I thought to regain credit by choosing the cheapest dishes. Wrong again. The Chairman was bemused by my choice of egg mayonnaise for starters and pressed me to change my mind but, fearing that would show indecisiveness, I stuck to my guns. So, while he ate his smoked salmon, I ate my egg mayonnaise.

On return to the office, I was interviewed in turn by the directors in charge of the three interests of the company, mining in Nigeria, logging in Borneo and shipbroking. Not knowing which of the three was eyeing me for employment, I showed enthusiasm for all three with dwindling credibility. I was asked by the Nigeria man what I thought about working with black people. I told him I had no thoughts about working with black people: I did not know any black person and had never had anything to do with them. 'Quite so,' he murmured. The Chairman summed up and returned to the matter of the blazer: he assumed that I was only wearing it, he explained to his colleagues, as I was leaving for Spitsbergen that night. Finally, he said that they would let me know the outcome before I left so that I would not have to wonder about it during my months away. I hurried back to Luton, irritated at the waste of time, but there were lessons to be learned for the future: wear a suit and choose smoked salmon.

On return from Spitsbergen, I went to Cambridge to enquire at the Scott Polar Research Institute if there was any possibility of joining an expedition to the Antarctic. Alas, not; I did not have the professional qualifications required, even to work in the kitchen. The last flicker of my polar flame extinguished, I went on to the Appointments Board to remind them of my existence and see what leftovers there might be. I had, however, a card up my sleeve. Dr MacDonald had given me a contact in Shell which I had saved for after Spitsbergen.

I went to see the Shell man in a new off-the-peg suit from Burtons', fully prepared to eat smoked salmon. After a hearty start to the interview I sensed some reserve on the part of the interviewer, his eyes constantly returning to my chin. Aged twenty-three, I had at last been able to grow enough hair on my face while in Spitsbergen for a beard of which I was very proud. The beard was too wispy on the cheeks to be taken seriously so I had come down to a trimmed goatee, itself none too luxuriant. Nevertheless, I hoped it gave me a piratical air or perhaps that of a Spanish nobleman but, whether it was the absurdity of it or its impertinence, the meeting limped to a close. Shell did not employ men with beards.

The beard had to go, without too much regret, as there had been goat-whinnying taunts as well. However, I kept it on to the last minute and then shaved off only the beard, leaving the moustache. My next potential employer required a hand-written CV and statement of personal ambitions. I sent this off and duly reported to the office of a sugar broker in Mincing Lane in the City. Before him on his desk lay my letter, with a red ring round some mistake in the first paragraph. The mistake absorbed my interest, leaning forward and craning my neck to make out what was wrong. Whether it was due to this distraction or the mistake or the insincerity of my interest in sugar, I did not impress as a potential sugar broker.

Time was slipping by. I decided that I would take the first job offered whether I liked it or not and with this resolve I headed to interview with N.M.Rothschild & Sons for the position of Graduate Trainee. As I walked across the courtyard of New Court, the Rothschild enclave behind the Mansion House in the heart of the City of London, I wondered at my very presence in these august surroundings. However, I was received very courteously by the Personnel Manager, Mr Scott. He called in a colleague and the interview was so gentlemanly that it seemed not to be an interview at all. What was I to make of this? I hoped it was a good sign, and it was.

I started work in November 1953. I was put in Cashiers in the banking hall to form an overall idea of the workings of the bank. Jobs were found for me to do, ranging from the translation of a notice in Spanish about the amortization of Chilean railway bonds, to the task of counting a sackful of the old small silver threepenny bits which had come in from West Africa. The banking hall was open-plan and sound was lost in the high ceiling with only a buzz to be heard. On one wall, an open fire blazed and the general atmosphere was that of gentleman's club. The lavatory was splendid, with very large washbasins with very large taps and bottles of gentlemen's lotions. You could clean your shoes there as many did, popping in as six o'clock approached to tidy up before going home. Gentlemanly hours too, ten to six, much appreciated by me commuting from Luton. There were fun and games at Christmas. The Chief Cashier wearing a railway guard's cap blew a whistle and waved a flag to signal the closure of the till, and lots were drawn to decide who would go into the Partners' Room wearing a novelty attachment to the shoe showing the upper peeling away from the sole.

After Christmas I was moved to Private Accounts. Here a new world opened up for me but once the novelty had worn off, I found the job created for me very unsatisfying. It was to enter in large leather-bound ledgers the stock-market transactions of the twenty or so private account holders and to apportion their dividend payments. All that was required for this work was neat handwriting and elementary arithmetic, a task performed before my arrival by the individual account keepers as part of their day-to-day duties. I was surplus to requirements, an imposition, but they took me to their hearts and I found them genial colleagues.

One day, Mr Clinch, the Head of the Department, sent me down to the Partners' Room with a letter requiring the signature of the senior partner. Through the glass panel of the door I saw that Mr Anthony, the style in which partners were known, was 'free'. I knocked, went in, presented the letter for signature, and dropped it off at Posts. Barely back at my desk, the telephone rang. It was Mr Scott, the Personnel Manager, asking if I could spare him a few moments. My heart leapt: was I about to be told of my move to another department? Instead, he asked if I had been down to the Partners' Room. Why yes, I said. Did you go straight in? Why yes, I said, amazed at the speed news travelled in Rothschilds. Mr Scott continued sternly 'in future you will wait until beckoned.'

This indeed was the protocol and a not unreasonable one, as the partners could not deal with more than one visitor at a time. At the end of the day, however, it gave rise to unseemly jostling as staff with letters to be signed competed to be beckoned. To catch the eye of Mr Eddy, who sat at the far end of the long room, it was necessary to screw the head hard right and, with cheek pressed to the glass, lock eyes on the target for a fear of missing the nod. Only two people were allowed to go in unbeckoned: the Chief Clerk and the Butler, the latter, it was commonly believed, with racing tips.

Life at Rothschilds was very agreeable. I settled in and set about conforming to type. Enjoying my new relative affluence, I opened a budget account at Austin Reeds and got measured up for a dark suit. I bought the approved pinstripe collarless shirts with separate stiff white collars and chose a few discreetly flashy ties to give myself character. I got shoes of the appropriate design, an umbrella, of course, and a curly-brimmed bowler with the fashionable fuzzy look. We had the most generous luncheon vouchers in the City and I made friends with other young bloods over Dover sole. The only discordant factor was Luton. Return there at the end of the day exposed me to the taunts of uncouth youths with their Charlie Chaplin imitations.

There were benefits galore: turkey at Christmas, holiday money, honeymoon money, and best of all, the annual bonus. I received my first bonus after I had been there six weeks and, not knowing then about the bonus system, was amazed that my menial work had found such early favour. Once a year there was the outing to Exbury, Mr Eddy's estate, for the annual cricket match. We were taken there and back from Waterloo by a Rothschild Special direct to Exbury Halt and thence by coach to the estate. Mr Eddy, already in his white flannels and striped cap, welcomed us and announced to dutiful applause that we were shortly to lunch on salmon. The cricket match had to be handled carefully so that the Exbury team captained by Mr Eddy won by a small margin.

What had I to worry about? I was working for the most prestigious bank in the City and could look forward to a good and very comfortable future. The only thing that was wrong was the work I was doing. After a year in Private Accounts, I went to see Mr Scott to remind him of the plan to move me round the office to gain experience. He replied that I must be patient. He was confident that I would rise to a managerial position in time: did I know how long Mr Clinch had been in Private Accounts? I shook my head. Twenty-one years. That made my mind up. I went round to the City of London Appointments Board and told them what I was looking for.

There was one possibility close at hand. The Newfoundland Corporation had an office in Rothschilds. I went to see the man in charge, with whom I was on nodding terms, to ask if there were any prospects for me in Newfoundland. He replied that there was nothing he could do as the Corporation was an investment vehicle only and was not involved in operations. A dead end.

The first of the appointments arranged by the City of London Appointments Board arrived. It looked unpromising but I nevertheless went for interview during my lunch break to the offices in Victoria Street of a company whose business was the manufacture of springs for rolling stock. The walls of the waiting room were hung with pictures of trains and photographs of springs and the interview was soon over. The next appointment looked even more unpromising as I could see no future for myself in Cherry Blossom Shoe Polish. As I was concealing my job hunting, I requested that the interview take place after work and thus made my way to an address in Park Royal in the early evening. The building was in total darkness apart from one window behind which my wretched interviewer was waiting. At the end of the rather irritable interview he asked if I had any comment on their product. I gave him the truth: the tins were hard to open despite the fiddly lever.

I kept an eye on the Situations Vacant column in the Times and one opening came up that looked quite promising. The Concessionary

Agent of the Peruvian Government was seeking to recruit an Assistant who would command a starting salary of £700 pa, which was substantially more than I was earning. I wrote off and was excited to be called to interview. The man I met was a Mr Siddiq, which was a bit of a surprise as I had expected to see a City gent or a Peruvian or at least someone from South America. Mr Siddiq was very nice and charming, and over dinner he told me all the exciting things I would be involved with if selected.

A few days later I received a letter offering me the job. I wrote back accepting it and went to see Mr Scott to give notice. He listened to my description of the job and asked if I would like the Bank to make enquiries about Mr Siddiq. Of course, I confidently agreed and was called back a day or two later to be told by Mr Scott, 'We have looked into your Mr Siddiq and our advice is that you should not take this job. He wishes to use you as a man of straw.' I had no wish to be a man of straw and, crestfallen and embarrassed, I returned to my desk in Private Accounts.

Time passed. The telephone on my desk rang. It was the Newfoundland man: could I pop down? Was there an opening in Newfoundland after all? No, but he asked me why I wanted to move, and we talked about my wish to work abroad, to use my languages and to travel. At length, he said that he was sure I would find something suitable and asked what I was going to say when I got back to my office. I replied that no one was aware of this or my earlier visit to him. If asked, I would say that I had come to enquire about possible openings in Newfoundland. Capital, he said, that's very good. I returned to my office pleased, but puzzled, by his interest.

A week or so later I received a letter headed Intelligence Coordination Staff inviting me to come for interview. Things were looking up. The interview took place in an office near Buckingham Palace. The interviewer, a very quiet and serious man, described how the work involved posting to an Embassy but seemed quite unable to say what the actual work was. The nearest he got to it was to say that its aim was to 'get under the skin of the country'.

Over that hurdle, I went on to a one-day assessment course

attended by two other postulants I never saw again. To put our analytical capability to the test, we were asked to allocate housing to demobilised servicemen according to rank and number of dependents. Just before pencils down, I realised that I had failed to take account of one of the criteria. I put a line through my whole answer and, in the few minutes remaining, managed to house one ex-sergeant-major with three children in a corner property. We were interviewed by a psychiatrist and at the end asked to write a short description of an event. My mind went blank. In desperation, I wrote down a joke and hoped it would do; if not, they might get a laugh out of it.

I did not think I had done at all well but I seemed unstoppable. Only the Final Board stood in my way. At some point, I had filled in a form in which I stated under "Reading" that I took the Times and the Economist. The latter was not true and I had to do some reading to prepare for the expected question. Over that hurdle, I was next asked what I thought was the significance to the West of Russian defectors. The answer I gave in desperation missed the point completely; clutching at a passing straw I said that defectors were 'plaster flaking off the monolith'. I passed the Board. Years later, I asked one of the Board members why I had been selected. He replied that I had given a brilliant answer to the question about defectors.

I handed in my notice again. Mr Scott was quite unperturbed and, if he had any feelings about me or my departure, he did not show them. I had to endure a month of leg pulling about MI5, and when my last day arrived Mr Clinch shook my hand warmly and I was taken for a night out by the rest of Private Accounts. The party broke up around midnight in Trafalgar Square and, left alone, I sat for a while on the steps. I had got what I wanted but it was a wrench to leave Rothschilds. They had been so good to me and though dissatisfied with my job I had enjoyed my time there and the companionship of my colleagues.

Training and Greece

On the 1st of September 1955, my twenty-fifth birthday, I went to sign on with my new employer. I was still, naively, under the impression that it was the Intelligence Coordination Staff. Pen in hand, I was asked if I was quite happy to sign on the dotted line. Why should I not be, I asked? The person dealing with me pressed on: do you know what organisation this is? No, I said, the penny still would not drop. It is the Secret Service. Ah, I said and signed. Though maintaining composure, I marvelled at the sheer unlikelihood of it; it is not every day that you join the Secret Service. Along with the pleasure and the excitement the implications began to sink in: would I be up to it, had I bitten off more than I could chew? These doubts were not dispelled by the talks we were given during the training course by officers on mid-tour leave, perched on the edge of the desk, talking airily about their tasks in Singapore and Berlin, or by Directors describing their responsibilities: how did they get to possess such personal projection or rise to such eminence?

I also felt that as an ex-bank clerk, I did not cut much of a figure among my fellow new entrants: a lawyer, a journalist, a half colonel, and a man who spoke Tibetan. However, group dynamics came into play and we soon became a happy band committing ourselves seriously to the training without becoming too serious about it. Our military colleague, older than us and destined for an administrative appointment, maintained an air of amused detachment.

The Head of Training opened the course with fine words. He stressed the need for intelligence officers to be inconspicuous, which we found ironic as he sported a maroon fedora. In the classroom we were taught all the tricks of the trade: agent management, rendez-vous arrangements (RV), surveillance and countersurveillance, recognition signals, passwords, dead letter boxes (DLB) and so forth. In the practical exercises, however, theory seemed to go out of the window so often that I concluded that it was part of the training to face us with hard-to-handle situations. For example, in my first RV exercise, I was to contact an 'agent' wearing a red scarf at the entrance to Horse Guards in Whitehall at 1.30pm. At the appointed time I stood among the spectators on the look-out for my man. Ten minutes late, a madman with open mac billowing, red scarf trailing, sun-glasses with one lens missing, raced past in the road. When I caught up with him he burst out laughing. Another 'agent' started shouting and attracted a crowd when I turned up without instructions for his evacuation by submarine.

The surveillance and countersurveillance exercises all descended into a high-speed chase however decorously we started. We chased each other through the Army and Navy stores and into the Catholic bookshop next door and out of its backdoor. After a nun was sent flying, the shop was placed out of bounds. We were set to clear a DLB and, here again, I supposed that there were lessons to be learnt from their preposterous locations. The DLB I had to clear was pinned to a notice board on the third floor of Scotland Yard. A fellow trainee was set to clear his from under the mat outside the door of the Turkish baths in Jermyn Street on which the commissionaire stood.

However, it was not all high jinks. We took part in three-day exercises in which we had to set up base in an unfamiliar part of London and pursue a developing narrative, nasty surprises included. It was not a pass/fail course and, at its end, we were assigned our first desk jobs. Raring to go, I was disappointed with mine: it was to study the French Communist Party, mainly through the media, looking out for signs of deviation from its hard-line Stalinist position. To provide relief from close reading of L'Humanité, the party newspaper, I had also to keep an eye on the Spanish and Portuguese communist parties. There were occasional visits by desk officers in MI5 on pretexts so thin as to suggest the need to get out of the office for a break. One visitor was a Cornishman by the name of U'ren. The guard at the front desk took a great delight in his visits and would call me on the telephone, 'a Mr Urine to see you, sir'.

I shared the office of a genial colleague whose task it was to keep an eye on me as well as on the German Communist Party. He had served in the Lagos Station during the war and had many a tale to tell of the confusion and disorder of those days, in which the writer Graham Greene was a willing participant under his self-designated cover appointment as Assistant Boom Defence Officer in Freetown. Nearly all the officers over the age of thirty had played some intelligence role during the war, which left those of us who had not feeling rather out of it. Service as an evacuee did not qualify.

After a year, the new entrants were all sent off for language training, two to Hong Kong for Chinese, two to learn Arabic at the Middle East Centre for Arab Studies (MECAS) in Lebanon, while I was to learn Greek on an MoD course for Army officers destined for Cyprus. The officers came from various military backgrounds and had volunteered for a variety of motives: young hotheads seeking action, a major wanting a change from running an Army store, a passed-over captain hoping to improve his chances.

The course was run by Julian Pring, a languid academic with a mocking glint in his eye, supported on Friday afternoons by the impatient Professor of Modern Greek at King's College, London. As the weeks passed, the varying levels of ability became evident and it was clear that the effect of the course, whatever may have been its initial ambition, would be to provide the officers with 'some Greek'. I left the course at the Christmas break and for the next few months

I had a daily two-hour lesson with Mrs Pring, who was Greek, with incidental conversation with her mother. I borrowed a tape recorder from the office to work on my accent. After eight or nine months' tuition I was tested by a Greek speaker at the office. He pronounced me 'excellent'; I was flattered but not deceived.

By now I had a wife and had left Luton behind. I married Madge Starmer, whom I had met and courted at Cambridge, during my time at Rothschilds and, with their honeymoon grant, we set off on an exhausting tour of Italy by train. After a few days at Rapallo, a suitable romantic resort on the Ligurian coast, we headed south via Pisa to Rome and Naples and then, bizarrely, across to Bari on the Adriatic coast and north to Rimini. Meant to be an exploratory trip to Italy, instead it explored the limits of endurance. We returned with relief to our bedsitter at 95 St George's Square, SW1, the best address I ever had, at £3 15 shillings a week.

I had to learn to drive. My instructor was a man of few words, uttered with laboured patience. When the needle crept up towards 30 mph he would say wearily, 'Thank you, Mr McDonald. We can't all be Stirling Moss.' One day, following to the letter his instruction to turn left at the next turning, I found myself driving round the parade ground of the Duke of York's barracks amid marching soldiers. 'Thank you, Mr McDonald. We don't want to join the Army today.' I passed my driving test despite reversing with the handbrake on. I bought a car and so became the first car owner in the family. It was a 1936 Ford 8, price £30, with a hole in the floorboard but, as the advert said, a good little runner. It was quite normal to see cars of such vintage on the roads.

I decided to take my wife to Barcelona to recapture my heady days. After adjusting one front brake to ensure even braking, we set off on an arduous journey of three days, top speed not much more than 40 mph, sleeping in the car. We stayed in a small hotel off the Ramblas but the magic had gone. After our return, I was stopped by the police who found that the front brakes did not work. The adjustment made before setting off to Barcelona had slackened off the only working front brake so we had driven some 2,000 miles without any front brakes. I was taken to court but let off with stern words.

We flew to Athens on 7th July 1956. Hot and confusing hours followed as we were shunted here and there, shaking hands with a stream of unknown people. Finally, we were deposited in a flat high on the slope of Lycabettos, the hill that tops the fashionable area of Kolonaki. Athens lay spread before us, and in the hot night the voice of Maria Callas floated on the still air from the ancient theatre below the Acropolis. Idyllic, a dream ending to our first day in Greece. We got up the following morning covered in bites. I assumed that they were mosquito bites but found that the bed was infested with bed-bugs.

Our Athens life began. A car collected us, taking me to the office and my wife to be looked after by colleagues' wives. On the training course there had been 'Life on a Station' lectures and here, at last, was I on a station. It was not what I expected. We were not tucked away in some quiet corner of the Embassy but housed across the road from it in a separate building. Including me, the station had seven officers, five secretarial staff, home-based security guards and a garage manned by two mechanics. The work of the station was dominated by the Cyprus question, the demand for self-determination and unification with Greece promoted by the terrorist organisation EOKA and Archbishop Makarios. The street in which the office was situated had been renamed with that of an EOKA 'martyr' and the station was under surveillance by KYP, the Greek Security Service, though liaison between us continued on matters unrelated to Cyprus.

I had to have a cover job in the Embassy and the slot chosen for me was that of Assistant Archivist, a lowly function without diplomatic protection. I had a suitably modest car for this rank, because as a junior officer, I qualified only for an entry-level vehicle and the car selected for me by Head Office was a Ford Prefect. Advised that a sun-visor was a worthwhile addition, I agreed, only to discover that I was the sole owner of a Ford Prefect in Athens, let alone one with a sun visor. With its foreign mission number plate it stood out, but given my modest role it mattered little.

We found a nice house with a garden in the village of Psychiko on the outskirts of Athens and took on a maid named Andromeda. We began to develop a social life; we went to the beach, explored ancient Athens, visited Delphi and so on, wanting for nothing. On October 26th, the name day of Dimitra, our first daughter was born.

About six months into my time in Greece, KYP dropped a bombshell: they requested the departure of an officer with the threat of formal expulsion if he was not withdrawn. The officer in question, an Alexandrine Greek with a wartime service background, ran the agents reporting on the Cyprus question and his loss was a heavy blow. Apart from the disruption of casework, there were security concerns associated with the handover which KYP no doubt hoped to exploit. Who was to take over the cases? It had to be a Greek speaker which reduced the options to three: the locally-engaged administration officer, a British Army veteran who had settled in Greece after the war, with working Greek but no operational experience; a colleague in his forties with a classical background and more than enough Greek but in manifestly poor health; and a probationer with burgeoning Greek but no operational experience.

The choice fell on me and, in a sense, I was in place as a reserve. Certainly, H/Athens, the Head of Station, had encouraged me to get out of the office to explore and immerse myself in my surroundings. I had needed no encouragement as it fed into my dream of language and place, of becoming invisible. I already had a suit made in the local style for which I chose only the cloth, leaving the rest to the tailor. I looked like a small-time gangster in it and at the end of my time in Greece I offered the suit to the office as operational stores.

I studied the cases and the operational arrangements. I had been under surveillance quite openly from the time of my arrival and simply ignored it, but now it was a different matter. The departing officer took me in hand. He had a Jaguar and relied on turn of speed, whereas I had my Ford Prefect and, unable to outrun my pursuers, had to rely on guile for which the small car was an advantage. It was nondescript, manoeuvrable and its 1200cc engine, tuned by the station garage, could deliver a fine burst of speed.

I was put to the test in a trial RV. I took anti-surveillance precautions, parked the car, and took up position at the pick-up point. After ten minutes I aborted and returned to the station where my mentor was waiting. He was not pleased; I had failed to shake off my pursuers. It was a hard lesson. Fortunately for us, KYP's surveillance capability was limited, it was not a sophisticated multi-car radio-controlled operation. Once they were lost, they were lost. You had to trust to it and had to act on it but, at the back of the mind, there always lurked the fear that you were mistaken, which kept the adrenalin flowing.

The hand-over took place. I now had three agents to look after whose safety depended on me. For meetings with them, I allowed myself two hours to lose the surveillance and, once satisfied, went to ground, usually in a cafe, until the time came to move when I checked again. I met one of the agents on the street. I had my Greek suit, was small with black hair and moustache and passed well enough for Greek. The second agent I picked up in my car; for the third, the arrangements were more complicated. As he was in an exposed position, an additional layer of security was built into the meeting arrangements. This was the use of an unattributable car, rented by the Station in a separate operation, which I picked up after shaking off surveillance from an agreed parking place, to which I returned it after the meeting. If I had documentary material to deposit, I stopped by the office, sometimes picking up a Station secretary on the way to assist in processing the material and drafting reports. I was usually out three nights a week, sometimes more, each contact taking several hours. I ran these agents for some two years right to the end of my time in Greece.

As time went by, personal relations with the surveillance team developed, reflecting the ambivalence of the relationship with KYP. Though my pursuers were serious in intent there was no personal animosity and when I was at home they parked quite shamelessly outside the house. We exchanged greetings when I came out and sometimes I sent Andromeda, the maid, to put them on ten minute notice. I think they were quite proud of my ability to give them the slip. They worked out one of the dodges I used and were waiting for me when I appeared, leaning out of their car and waving.

We had occasional intelligence coups, the most striking but pointless of which was to obtain details of the Zurich Agreement on Cyprus before the Ambassador had received the text on his own channels. This was the achievement of the agent I met on the street and his report in translation was uncannily close to the text of the Agreement. At our next meeting I remarked on this and he explained that he had a photographic memory. He was very proud of this and pressed me to come to his house so that he could demonstrate it. Exceptionally, an occasion was arranged and at his house I took down a book from his shelves and chose a page for him to read. Hours later, after a meal, we returned to the page which he recalled with few errors. It was a remarkable performance and an admirable ability, especially in an agent.

With the ending of the conflict, surveillance ceased within weeks and attention turned to the short-lived political ambitions of General Grivas, the leader of EOKA, who had set himself up in Athens.

The demands of my work affected but did not close down life outside it. In the tense political atmosphere, the expatriate community continued to dwindle and from a departing American I clubbed together with two friends to buy a yacht for $1,000, about £300 each. It was a handsome vessel, a 30 ft Bermuda-rigged sloop, berthed at the Turkolimano marina in Piraeus. Soon after acquiring it, I and a fellow admiral, as we called ourselves, decided one weekday afternoon to take the boat out for a sail. Failing to register that no one else was out sailing, we shot out of the harbour in a brisk breeze experiencing for the first time the enormous pull exerted by a boat of this size under sail. We were soon in difficulties and tacked to and fro to regain the harbour but we lacked the skill to negotiate the marina entrance in the adverse wind and surrendered ourselves to beaching ignominiously at the foot of the bay.

Because I had to be on call, I could not get away to join my fellow admirals on long trips but I sailed to and from the nearby islands and took part in one three-day visit to the island of Hydra, an immensely satisfying experience. Sunday picnics to Aegina, the nearest island to Piraeus, were popular with the secretaries and invitations to join the party were highly prized. It took an hour and more to get there where, anchored in a turquoise bay, we bathed beneath the remains of a temple on the headland.

I was alone for an extended period when my wife was in the UK for treatment of the depression into which she sank after the birth of our first daughter. The Embassy doctor had prescribed a newly available drug called Doriden whose unwelcome side effects were not yet recognised and she became addicted to it. In the UK, her treatment included ECT with its unwelcome after-effects. She returned to Athens the shell of the person she had been, her recent memory wiped out and prone to fits, and was soon back on anti-depressant medication. She nonetheless had a successful second pregnancy and gave birth to our second daughter in August 1959.

During her absence, I set off one Saturday morning to photograph the mimosa in full bloom at Nauplion and on the road I picked up a hitchhiker. He turned out to be a soldier heading home on leave and he insisted I accompany him to his home to meet his family. As it was not much out of my way, I allowed myself to be persuaded and so entrapped myself as the family would not let me go until the following afternoon. On the Sunday morning we drove to the great theatre of Epidaurus, not a soul was there, and took photographs of each other. Weeks later, a family of peasants turned up at the Embassy and I had to be summoned from across the road to remove them. I took them to see the Acropolis which none of them had ever visited.

Greece, wonderful country. In all our time there we were not faced with any personal animosity, despite horrific reports from Cyprus, and were privileged to enjoy the last days of pre-mass tourism. It all had to end though and in January 1960 we sailed home in style on the SS Stratheden, out of Bombay bound for London. Thanks to our infant daughters, we were allocated a state room with square windows and walnut woodwork and beds to the irritation of the Air Attache, a rather grand Air Commodore, in his first class cabin with pipes and bunks and measly porthole. An Assistant Archivist… really!

Venezuela

The Stratheden docked at Tilbury. My brother was there to meet us and took us in his huge Austin Princess, a used car bargain, to Bexleyheath where my parents were back in their own house twenty years after the wartime dispersal of the family. Our arrival doubled the size of the household and the question of who slept where was resolved by the three sons sleeping in the sitting room. It worked well enough once we had settled into the routine of making and unmaking the beds, which could not be left in place as they took up most of the floor area.

My father had transferred from Vauxhall Motors in Luton to the London office of General Motors and my mother was working as cashier at the Arts Theatre restaurant, across the road from Leicester Square tube station. Her work affected our night-time arrangements as she had to sit behind the till until the restaurant closed and did not get to Bexleyheath station until well past eleven o'clock. My brother picked her up in the Princess or not, as sometimes she fell asleep on the train and was carried on to Gillingham. On those occasions, she would go to the Police Station which would telephone for someone to come and fetch her. One night, waiting with lights off outside the Co-op near Bexleyheath station, the police pounced on my brother suspecting him of some nefarious purpose and refused to accept his explanation until a tiny figure in hat, coat and handbag tottered round the corner. It was pure Ealing comedy. 'Is this a heist, boys?'

I reported to the Office and learned that my next job was to be staff officer to the Vice-Chief. I was taken aback. This was a far cry from reading l'Humanité and was surely an excessive and alarming reward for my performance in Athens which I, with my worm's eye view of my prospects in the Service, saw as no more than doing what was required of me. Without the experience needed for the appointment, I went as a lamb to slaughter to take over from a man ten years older who revelled in the scope of the job and who was leaving the Service to go into politics. An avalanche of responsibilities and unfamiliar work descended on me. I saw the whole Service at work and its place in Whitehall and had a ringside seat at the denouement of the George Blake affair.

The Vice-Chief was an austere and rather forbidding Scot who did not suffer fools at all. His sense of humour occasionally broke the surface and there were those he viewed with enough favour to invite to lunch at the YMCA in Tottenham Court Road. It was a bracing experience preceded by a swim and followed by a brisk walk back to the office 'to stir up the phagocytes'. There were eight of us, four officers and four secretaries, in the guarded enclave of the Chief. We had our own lavatories. I dreaded coinciding with the Chief and was horrified one day to find the great man at the urinal. Escape impossible, I took up position at his side in silence, neither of us able to think of anything to say. In 1960, Head Office passes were introduced and the first number in the issue, 1000, was given to the Chief and the succeeding numbers down the line to me in seventh place, 1007. I was the envy of my colleagues. When showing the pass I nonchalantly covered the 1.

After fifteen months in the job, the Personnel Department, perhaps recognising that the appointment required a more experienced officer, asked what ideas I had about my next move. I replied that I would like to use my Spanish, and Personnel offered the choice between second officer in Caracas and opening a station in La Paz. I was sure that I did not have the experience and confidence to open a station and chose the Caracas appointment. I would be posted as Second Secretary and, to help me prepare for the meteoric rise from Assistant Archivist, I was given a Foreign Office booklet about the role of a Third Secretary on first appointment. Set in a bygone era it had become a laughing stock. It described the duties of an obsequious creep among which, for instance, was to ascertain the location of the lavatories before a reception at which he was to dance attendance on the Ambassador's wife, alert to her every need.

I ought to have paid less attention to the booklet's list of equipment needed by a diplomat as I spent most of the posting allowance at Bourne and Hollingsworths' buying a dinner service for twelve, cutlery, candlesticks, punchbowls and the like which have cluttered my baggage over the years, rarely used. I had to get a dinner jacket, which I bought off-the-peg from Moss Bros hire department. On top of all this, I now rated a Ford Zephyr. It was looking pretty good.

In May 1961, we sailed in grand style on the small one-class Oranje Nassau liner to La Guaira, the port serving Caracas. We left Southampton and crossed to a French port to pick up passengers. By the evening we were in the Bay of Biscay and, feeling unwell, decided to miss the Captain's Welcome on Board cocktails. A knock on the door. I answered it in my pyjamas: it was the Chief Steward. He said, 'The Captain is waiting'. I got dressed. As I approached the Captain, my hand held out, the Steward at his side said, 'What, no dinner jacket!'. That set the tone: we were to have a voyage in which the formalities were observed and all on board were expected to cooperate and take part in the hoop-la and shuffleboard competitions. The Last Night of the Ocean Crossing was the occasion for a banquet with extravagant sugar confections and the British Ambassador-designate to Costa Rica, deemed to be the doyen of those on board, was called upon to give a speech of appreciation.

After calls at Barbados, the Dutch colony of Aruba and Trinidad we finally reached La Guaira, by repute hotter than at the Equator a few degrees to the south. We were driven up to Caracas, half an hour by motorway, and were taken to the Rio Azul, an attractive colonial-style hotel. I telephoned H/Caracas to let him know we had arrived and he came round to say hello. He was a tall, self-consciously good-looking man; confident, elegant, and suave, he was my polar opposite. As we sat sipping drinks in the courtyard of the hotel, I felt that I was the underling in a remake of Our Man In Havana.

We had a restless night at the Rio Azul, disturbed every now and then by thuds on the roof caused, I learned in the morning, by falling avocados. Any romantic notion I had about Caracas was quickly dispelled. There were no sleepy colonial buildings with muleteers in ponchos and sombreros loafing in the shade. Caracas was a brash noisy city of high-rise buildings through which flyovers twisted. The first few days were the usual nightmare of house finding and introductions. We settled on a villa in an unexpected leafy quarter, a kind of diplomatic compound with lawns and trees with orchids, a haven of peace. At 3,000 ft Caracas was cool at night.

There was nothing grand about the Embassy which was simply a rented office in a high-rise building difficult to find in a city without landmarks. The Ambassador was Sir Douglas Busk who in the inter-war years had been a leading British Alpinist. He welcomed me as a fellow climber and co-opted me in the party he was putting together to climb Pico Bolivar, Venezuela's highest mountain. He showed me the letter he had written to the Venezuelan Mountaineering Club, outlining his plan and seeking advice about guides and mules, and the reply he had received. In it, the writer welcomed the Ambassador's interest and enthusiasm but, with respect, felt obliged to point out to His Excellency that there was a cable-car that would take him to the summit. The Ambassador snorted with rage.

The Caracas station consisted of H/Caracas, Secretary and now me. I was given two cases to take over. The first was a senior British businessman, long resident in Caracas and embedded in the political and business nexus. In years gone by, he had been valuable because of his personal connection with the then President whom he had come to know when both were students at Madrid University. However, he had long ceased to be an agent of influence, to use the jargon, but remained a useful contact. I had lunch with him at his opulent residence. I was shown by a servant to my place halfway down a long table but, unable to make out my host's murmurings, I unceremoniously picked up my plate and dragged my chair to his side. What he had to say was of interest to me as a newcomer but it was not reportable intelligence. In fact, it was only towards the end that we ventured into intelligence territory when he asked if we could mount a technical operation against his Venezuelan partner whom he suspected of cheating him.

The other case was a British journalist in his thirties stringing for a British newspaper, who had been put in place by the Service to cover the activities of Dominican exiles conspiring to overthrow President Trujillo. H/Caracas warned me that he was 'rather wild'. When I went to see him he opened the door with a hammer in his hand, a precaution, he explained, as in his work unwelcome curiosity attracted unwelcome attention. I did not doubt it because Caracas was a dangerous city where everyone was at risk of being caught up in a gun battle in the supermarket. In addition to physical confidence, he had the mental resilience to cope with the stress of keeping afloat with the thinnest of cover in an area of peripheral British interest. There was an element of showmanship in his behaviour: he enjoyed being a tough guy.

I took to him instantly. He was about my age and build, our backgrounds were similar and he was a rock climber. I cannot recall that he ever told me anything of intelligence significance about the Dominican dissidents; I went to see him primarily to enjoy his company. Beer in hand, we listened to and endlessly replayed a recording of the Red Army choir and he recounted stories of his rascally boyhood in Liverpool. On one visit, I found a friend of his there, an air hostess overnighting in Caracas. When the drinks ran out, he simply stepped over the balcony wall and disappeared from view. Leaning over the balcony, we watched him climb down the face of the building and come back up with a bag of bottles in his teeth, by which time occupants of the building were also leaning over their balconies to watch 'el Inglès' climbing again. The flat was on the seventh floor. He could not resist showing off.

After return from Caracas I kept up with him for a while. I bought and sent him climbing gear from Robert Lawrie's shop and followed up the introduction he gave me to Gwen Moffat, a leading woman climber he had known in his Welsh climbing days. He also gave me the telephone number of Josephine who ran a dirty postcards shop near Putney Bridge with whom I had a couple of boozy sessions. However, as is the way of the world, our contact died away but he remains vivid in my memory.

Many years later, I read in a book of climbing memoirs the story of an unknown man who walked into a Llanberis pub, a climbers' haunt, seeking a guide to take him up the Master's Wall, then regarded as the hardest climb in Wales. This had a characteristic flavour: was this man the daredevil journalist of my Caracas days, David Nott? I do not know, but he can now be named as he has published an account of his thirty-year intelligence career entitled Memoirs of an MI6 Agent. In his book, he refers to his case officers as hard taskmasters, which hardly described our meetings. He is perhaps best known for his climbing exploits in Venezuela, which he has described in two books.

Aside from work, there was little to distract or entertain. Caracas was disappointing. Surprisingly, we were not entertained by colleagues at the Embassy; no invitations from the Ambassador or even from H/Caracas. There was none of the usual fuss made of a newly-arrived wife. It was as if all were afflicted by a kind of Caracas ennui. There was nothing to do. We took the children to a park and found it deserted apart from a two-toed sloth without a tree to climb and a man selling 'pajaritos', little paper birds on a string with wings that flapped when whirled round. We explored the road leading out of Caracas to the south only to find it end abruptly at the jungle. There were no beach parties. It was far too hot down on the coast, the water was muddy from the outflow of the Orinoco and swimming was dangerous in the waves rolling off the Atlantic. Shopping afforded no distraction. In the cold supermarkets huge butterflies flapped hopelessly up and down the aisles. Our bijou enclave was hushed and discreet, no sign of life, no noisy neighbours.

All this and boredom fed the depression of my wife and she grew anxious about her pregnancy. At very low ebb, she was admitted to hospital where she gave premature birth by Caesarean section to a son. Such was her condition that the Embassy, in consultation with the doctors, judged that any treatment she might require was best provided in the UK. We were given marching orders and within a week we flew back to London after barely six months in Caracas. On arrival mother and baby were whisked off to the Maudsley Hospital and I, with my daughters aged two and four, was sent on leave to sort out our affairs.

Introduction to Africa

Sorting ourselves out meant going back to live in Bexleyheath once again. There was no alternative: my wife was in hospital; we had no place of our own and, even if we had, paying someone to help run the house and look after the children was beyond my means. I had run up a bill of several hundred pounds in hotel and other costs in the week following our return and had to ask the Office for a loan. The burden of looking after us fell once again on my uncomplaining parents.

I reported back to work crestfallen, my tail between my legs, expecting reproach. None came, there was not a single word of the criticism I felt I deserved. I had known very well that my wife was not fit to be posted but had hoped that the larger life abroad with servants would have lifted her out of her depression. I was wrong and had blotted my copybook.

After a few weeks in a temporary job, I was posted to the section dealing with stations in Southern Africa as assistant desk officer. The desk officer was Daphne Park, not long back from the Congo, where she gained a celebrity status such that mention of her name was followed by 'of the Congo'. Weary of hearing this, the Director for Africa observed how nice it would be to hear of her in some other context, say, as an authority on Spode china.

Who and Why and Where and What was this remarkable woman? One book has been written and another is under way about her life, her war service, her SIS career, her onward march through the BBC to Somerville College and eventually to the House of Lords. That was all to come. To me she was simply a colleague, open and friendly, even motherly. She was bursting with energy and was forever bustling along the corridor to the Director to seek approval for some project or to protest at one being turned down. When she pushed her glasses up the bridge of her nose, I knew she was in battle mode.

I now had to learn about Africa. I knew of course about the struggles for independence but nothing about Africans themselves as distinct from those portrayed in popular culture. I took part in a seminar organised by the Foreign Office about African culture and pre-colonial history, which was all very interesting and useful background but it gave little idea about how to deal with Africans themselves. But my mentor was at hand. Daphne loved to reminisce and relive her time in the Congo: Mobutu this, Lumumba that and Tshombe the other. Her Ambassador was very supportive but nevertheless argued that much of what she learned was not, strictly speaking, secret intelligence and crossed over into Embassy reporting. They came to the practical if unorthodox arrangement that whatever Daphne learned after 11pm was intelligence.

I was at her flat one evening. The telephone rang: it was Cyrille Adoula, the Congolese Prime Minister, calling from Brussels, asking for a meeting. Daphne was in difficulty as she was under a Foreign Office ban on unauthorised meetings with her Congolese contacts for fear of 'muddying policy waters' but Adoula required an answer. Daphne looked at me and, raising her arms in a gesture of helplessness, agreed to his request.

The powers that be decided that I had not enough to do and I was in addition appointed assistant desk officer for stations in East and West Africa, and it was in that capacity that I had my first dealings with an African, a French-speaking Togolese businessman. This man was a contact of the station covering Ghana which was obliged to operate from

Lome, the capital of neighbouring Togo, because of the ban placed by the Commonwealth Relations Office on the Secret Intelligence Service (SIS) entering the newly independent African countries. H/Lome had worked up contact with the Togolese whose business took him into Ghana. I was charged to look after him for a day.

I decided that a visit to Windsor would be a suitable start to the day, despite the rain. I picked him up at his hotel and drove slowly through congested traffic to Windsor where, at last, with a wave of the hand I pointed to the castle. He had fallen silent during the drive. I asked him if he would like to see the castle. No, he said, let us return to London. What to do next? I racked my brains during the grim ride back and decided to take him for tea to the Lyons Corner House at Marble Arch, hoping somehow that it would impress him. As we sipped tea, I asked him if he liked the place. No, he said, people are looking at me. I did not tell him that I was equally the object of interest and we left.

From remarks he made I got a glimmer of light: would he like to go to a striptease show? Alright, he said without excitement. Soho next and, after we had watched a couple of turns, I asked him if he liked the show. In the absence of any sign of animation, I knew the answer. He was as fed up as I was and, talking in the street outside, he came to the point, 'mes besoins sexuels' he said, my sexual needs. I took out the remaining money I had for his entertainment, pushed it down his breast-pocket, shook his hand and left him to it.

Another opportunity to hone my skills came with the arrival of three policemen from Mali. The hyper-active H/Lome, casting around for something to do, visited Bamako, the capital of Mali, and, carried away by the Third World enthusiasms of the Ambassador, offered to look after the policemen during their stay in London after the course with Bristol police they were to attend. Halfway through the course, one of the three announced that he wished to return home. He resisted giving a reason but finally said that it was due to constipation caused by the food in the Bristol Police canteen. Despite offers of treatment he was adamant and, after signing statement absolving everyone but himself, he was put on a plane.

My turn came when the remaining two came for their few days in London. I took them to watch the Trooping of the Colour from the Guards stand where we caused confusion by sitting in the American Ambassador's seats. I took them to Talk of the Town, the quasi-night club in a theatre. Sitting in the dress circle, we looked down on Sophie Tucker, straining to hear the words of 'Sophie's little lover pills'. We had our photograph taken, all three of us looking rather shiny.

The crowning experience of their stay was the farewell dinner. I went to pick them up from their hotel at the agreed time, and after I had waited twenty minutes in reception, one of the two appeared. I enquired after the other: 'He is saying his prayers', he said and went off, I assumed, to fetch him. After a further interval, he reappeared and said that they were unable to come to dinner with me. Pressed to explain why he eventually said, 'Nous venons de prendre notre laxatif.' Hints to Travellers: Malians, prone to constipation.

The time came for Daphne to return to the fray and, the CRO ban having been lifted, she was posted to Lusaka where, running true to form, she soon positioned herself at the political crossroads. Her successor was so totally unlike Daphne that I wondered if his appointment had been chosen deliberately for that reason. A cold-war veteran from Berlin, he took all Daphne's bubbling pots off the stove and set about reducing his workload to the minimum.

After some three years in my dual role it was my turn to move on and I was surprised to be posted to Beirut. Had Personnel forgotten Venezuela? They did not enquire about my wife's fitness for posting and I did not ruffle the waters as she was, in fact, well enough. In the aftermath of Caracas she remained in one hospital or another for several months. During this time I bought a house in Redhill and settled in with my parents as my mother was needed to look after the children. When my wife was eventually discharged, my parents moved out and she moved in and, though the black dog was never far away, we began a settled life that was to last several years.

Beirut

We opted to travel to Beirut by land and sea and in May 1964 set off with three excited children on a three-day drive to Venice. Our new car was a Hillman Minx, a prosaic vehicle lacking the panache of the Ford Zephyr, unavailable because of the blacklisting of Ford in Arab countries. In Venice we boarded the Ausonia, a small luxurious liner, for the voyage to Beirut. Life on board was very pleasant, with swimming for the children and excellent Parma ham for daddy. I chatted in French with a Lebanese lady and asked her if she spoke Arabic. Yes, she said, but only to the servants. On arrival in Beirut we were taken to the Mayflower Hotel in the fashionable Hamra district. It was hot and humid, though we were told that the city was only warming up for the summer.

Most Embassy staff lived in apartments and we looked at several but found them dark and airless, quite unsuitable for the children, then aged three, five, and seven. We were lucky to find a house with a garden, a rarity in Beirut, away from the busy centre in the Patriarchate district. It had three doors opening onto the street, each with its own separate number in the French fashion, a custard apple tree each side of the front door and a towering dusty bougainvillea at the end of the garden. Feral cats roamed the neighbourhood and, so we were told, kept the rats down. The house had ineradicable cockroaches which came out in force at night and before bed I indulged in a flurry of zapping. In the morning Behaya, our maid, swept up the remains, just husks as the juicy innards had been eaten, presumably by their fellows. We acquired a cook, Jacob, not a very good one despite the dogeared testimonials he presented. He had a limited repertoire and was one of those people who despite their best intentions and endeavours consistently get things wrong, sometimes spectacularly. Bringing up the dessert at one of our rare lunch parties, he tripped on the stairs and fell into the tart he was carrying. He entered the room, his white tunic smeared with orange goo, and served the rearranged tart. Nobody said a word.

We entered Embassy life. My wife, wearing hat and gloves as protocol still required, called on the wife of the Ambassador and we received invitations from colleagues. The lunch with the Counsellor was a scene from a satire on diplomatic life. During the meal, one of the guests commiserated with him over his recent illness, to which he replied that the absence from work had given him time to finish his piano concerto. After lunch we moved to the drawing room in which there was a small grand piano. Our host asked the Ambassador's secretary, who was among the guests, if she had time for a song. At this point, some of the guests hastily made their departure. With her hand on the piano and accompanied by the host she burst into a fruity contralto.

The Beirut station was large by Service standards. H/Beirut, the station commander, was Peter Lunn, a legendary Service figure, of whom it was said that he had three interests only: Intelligence, God, and Skiing, the last of which suggests that his posting to Beirut was not entirely coincidental. He could pursue all three interests every day: work in the morning, on the slopes in the afternoon and be back in time for Benediction. He had an analytical mind observable in his long step-by-step telegrams of one sentence paragraphs, which commonly extended beyond 'z', the alphabetical numbering used in those days of book and pad coding.

The officer I took over from had been a fellow new entrant and the handover of the two agents he was running was effected in a comradely spirit. In addition, he processed the confidential information obtained by the Oriental Counsellor at the Embassy, a splendid old habitué of the Lebanese salons. He bore the extraordinary name of Maroon Arab, which at first I took to be a pseudonym.

The first agent I took over was a Levantine Greek born in Damascus who spoke three languages, Arabic, Greek at home, and with me, French. He ran, or more precisely was the intermediary between, two sub-agents, one in Iraq and the other in Syria, both of whom reported by secret writing (SW). His role was to receive and pass on to me their communications and handle their rare visits. Towards the end of my time he spotted the sub-agent's name in the Deaths column of a Syrian newspaper. Then, weeks later, a further report arrived creating the impression that work continued on the astral plane, but it had evidently been held up in the post.

The other case was of a similar nature. The head agent was a former officer in the pre-war Yugoslavian army and the sub-agent an officer in the Syrian security service. The Yugoslav was a character out of a Dennis Ambler story. A rising Army officer at the outbreak of war, he stayed loyal to the King and was posted in an official capacity to Turkey where he joined in the wartime intriguing. One of his fellow conspirators was the Papal Nuncio who later became Pope John XXIII.

The agent's world fell apart when the Communists took power after the war and he was marooned in Turkey, forced to live off his wits. He claimed to have been recruited by Philby, whom he much admired and of whose integrity he remained unshakeably convinced. In Beirut, he was scraping a living, what we paid him part of it. I used to see him in his apartment and occasionally stayed for 'dîner et programme'. While the food was finishing off, he showed me his old uniforms and reminisced about his time at St Cyr, the French Sandhurst, and the welcome he received when he called on his old friend at the Vatican. After dinner came the programme, the showing of a pornographic film which we had to watch in play-back as well for some specious technical reason. I admired his resilience and that of the other agent whose situation was also precarious.

I recruited and ran two other agents, neither of whom lived up to their potential, one in the Lebanese Security Service, who proved to be in the wrong section to have access of interest, and the other who worked in the postal interception section of the Post Office. The latter had such bad eyesight that picking him up by car was like a training exercise gone wrong: I had to run after him as he picked his way along the street. I gave him names of interest and he brought letters addressed to them unopened which I said I would return in due course. 'Why?' he said, 'You can keep them.' No, they did not reseal opened letters and send them on, they just tore them up. That simplified matters but, in practice, we had made a rod for our back. The labour of processing the scrawled Arabic of these letters far outweighed the likelihood of finding anything useful.

Excitement: we had a walk-in, an Egyptian intelligence officer. Was it for real or was it a provocation? H/Beirut dealt with him and, to give time for enquiries, arranged an outside meeting a few days later. The Egyptian asked him for his name and, off the cuff, H/Beirut whimsically replied 'Captain Cook'. Head Office was displeased. It was forbidden to use names attributable to, for example, MPs, judges, members of the Armed Forces and so on and, to make matters worse, the Naval Attache at the Embassy in Ankara was a real-life Captain Cook. HO went into overdrive and quickly issued all members of the Service with an alias to use in an emergency. Mine was Quelrayn.

The Information Research Department of the FCO ran a mailing operation in which letters about British policy, in other words propaganda, were posted to persons of discernment in countries round the world. In a futile attempt to disguise provenance, the letters were sent to Embassies to post and several hundred of such letters, in identical cheap buff envelopes with addressograph addresses all over the Middle East, arrived by bag. The task of posting them was shared out

Aged about four recovered
from the illnesses of the
previous year.

Bexleyheath in the run up to World War II.
Off to school with my brother, aged eight and
seven, in our pullovers and knee-high socks
knitted by Mother.

Luton sixteen
years later. I am at
Rothschilds, my
brothers at university
and school. Mother
chirpy, Father not.

Above: Captain of Cross Country, centre front row. Atkinson third from the left in the back row.

Below: At the College door in the city of dreams. Cambridge 1952.

Aboard the Sysla, the Governor's yacht, heading for Prince Charles Foreland.

After landing on the first expedition. Alone with our boxes and without communications as the Sysla sails away.

Put ashore with the kayak and the boat which was to dominate the third expedition. Its fanciful name, Queen Elizabeth II, can just be made out. Image courtesy of Eve Leeds.

The plane-table survey of the first Spitsbergen expedition. In the background the Foreland Sound and the mainland.

Stand clear! The author, aged 19 and still growing up, strikes a pose.

Looking south along the central range, the backbone of the island.

Squelching through the soil
polygons on the Foreland plain.
Setting up a forward camp.

My fellow desperado.
Note the copycat waistcoat.

The very superior base hut of the third expedition built in the 1920s by the
Scottish Mining Syndicate.

Interior of the base hut drawn by me before packing up at the end of the third expedition. Note the square-toed boots.

London 1955.
The author as city dandy and
first wife Madge attend a wedding.

Wish you were here.
Writing a postcard
on honeymoon in Italy.

Greece 1959.
Visiting Epidaurus with the
Greek family that captured me.

Nothing escapes my gaze.
The gimlet-eyed H/Benghazi.

Benghazi. With the Consul-General in the temporary office in D'Aosta Barracks during the Six Day War.

The improvised sanatorium and patient in the Bekaa Valley high above Beirut.

By the front door of the Beirut house with the custard apple tree.

1968.
All aboard the Citta di Livorno bound for Tripoli.

The DG attends the equestrian display put on for
the visit of Prince Charles and Princess Diana.

Greeting the
Sultan
at a New Year's
Eve reception at
Seeb palace.

Shaking hands with
Vice-President Bush
at a State banquet.

In my office presenting Sue, my PA, with the commemorative medal
issued on the occasion of the twenty-fifth anniversary of the Sultan's accession.

Shooting the breeze with my son at Bustan Palace Hotel, near Muscat.

On the DG's dhow with Sue and the Head of Administration. That's the life!

Daughter's first rock-climb.
On a stance halfway up the
east face on Tryfan in North Wales.

Climbing visit to
the sea cliffs of Cornwall.

On Derbyshire limestone with Harry Woodbridge high above Matlock.

Woebegone with guide on the summit of Point Lenana, Mount Kenya.

Back down and recovered from altitude sickness.

Chamonix. Sue on the slab and in triumph at the top of the climb.

'Where does the route go next?'

Oman. Setting off with Tony Howard to open the route on Jebel Misht.
In its upper section it follows the shadowed crack to the right of the summit.
Image © Di Taylor.

On Vipère au Pied, an 800 ft climb on Barberine, a cliff near the Swiss border. A viper at your heel, indeed! in total contrast to....

Enough. My last climb a week before my eighty-eighth birthday ending seventy years on and off the rocks.

and, leaving the Embassy with my portion, I bumped into a member of the staff of the Regional Information Office, the section organising the posting operation, carrying his bundle of letters. Thinking to avoid using the same letter box, I asked him where he intended to post his letters. He was surprised: 'You don't really intend to post them, do you?' I asked him what he did with his. 'I throw them in the sea.'

Not regular members of Chancery, we were not on the merry-go-round of diplomatic entertaining though we were expected to lend a hand when the Embassy was the host, notably on the Queen's Birthday. In the afternoon, the British community piled in while in the morning, a vin d'honneur was held to which representatives of the government, embassies and other notables came. It was a colourful gathering, with the Armed Service attachés in comic opera uniforms and the Patriarchs of the various churches in their robes.

Ever mindful of the need to develop new contacts, I fell into conversation with the Consul of the Yugoslav Embassy. We got on well and he invited me to join him in a visit he was making after the vin d'honneur to a Yugoslav ship in port. To keep the pot bubbling I agreed with sinking heart and, many hours later, after a gruelling session on board the ship we arranged to keep in touch.

He telephoned one day and launched into a long confused description of a problem he was facing. He had been detailed to accompany his newly-arrived Ambassador to the presentation of credentials but did not possess the formal dress required. I said that I would see what I could do to help and found two Embassy colleagues who possessed the required dress. The Counsellor's trousers were about the right length but the coat too narrow at the chest for the well-built Yugoslav, while the Information Officer's trousers were far too long and the coat probably too big, but it was the best we could do. I took the mismatched coat and trousers to him and he put them on. The trousers came over his shoes and did not quite meet at the waist while the coat and sleeves were too long. He looked like a waiter in a Chaplin film. He sighed: 'Me voilà, vêtu comme un singe capitaliste,' dressed like a capitalist monkey.

Living in Beirut was easy once you had learned its ways and made allowances. Called the Paris of the Middle East, Beirut was certainly the most French city of the Middle East but there was no Montmartre or Champs-Élysées. It was a crowded, bustling, noisy, anything-goes kind of city where you might meet a service taxi driving in the wrong direction down a one-way street, with the driver half out of his seat, his door partially open to make room for an extra passenger.

The weather was agreeable most of the year and delightful in spring when Lebanon burst into bloom but in the hot summer months the climate was oppressive. The air was trapped by the mountains encircling the city and smog built up. Looking down from the mountains, Beirut lay under a brown cloud. Home-based staff were entitled to the quaintly-named Estivation Allowance with which to buy some relief from the heat. In our first summer we wasted it on a third share in a beach hut at a private beach. There were too many huts, too many people, too small a beach and a tepid sea. No relief: just sand and sweat.

To get away from the heat, we drove up to the Cedars of Lebanon at 9,000 ft on Mount Lebanon in the north of the country. The few remaining trees are the treasured successors of the forest mentioned in the Bible, cut down by the Phoenicians to build their ships. However, trees are trees and we soon lost interest. The most memorable part of the visit was the hair-raising drive down when the brakes failed. Unable to stop, I careered round the bends in first gear tugging at the handbrake.

At Easter we flew to Jerusalem. We lodged in the pilgrims' quarters (unheated) attached to St George's, the Anglican Cathedral, in the old part of the city. We meandered through the narrow streets to the holy sites, the Wailing Wall, the great Mosque and the Church of the Holy Sepulchre, where acolytes of the disputing Churches competed for our custom. We went to Jericho and Bethlehem and paddled in the Dead Sea. A memorable week, the children old enough to have a sense of the occasion.

As our second summer approached, my younger daughter began to have chest problems which developed into recurring attacks of bronchitis. Our Palestinian doctor, a former consultant paediatrician at Westminster Hospital, said that an air-conditioner was needed. I wrote to Head Office but they said that the Estivation Allowance was provided for such needs. I wrote again with a letter from the doctor saying that the child should be in a sanatorium with its mother, still to no avail.

After a renewed attack of bronchitis, I packed up what camping gear we had and drove up the Damascus road to Chtoura, a village at the edge of the Bekaa Valley. Finding a camp site with basic facilities, we set ourselves up under a vine-covered pergola within croaking distance of a frog farm. The air was dry and pure and the nights cool. Close at hand was Zahle with its restaurant famous for frogs' legs which they served heaped up in a pyramid to be eaten with fingers. At the head of the valley, at Baalbek, were the ruins of a huge Roman temple. Unrestored, the fallen masonry lay amid the vegetation, sections of huge pillars evoking Shelley's Ozymandias, 'Two vast and trunkless legs of stone…'

I drove down to work in the morning and back up at lunchtime and up and down again in the evening as work required. One evening I took a prescription for my daughter to a chemist. The proprietor sat at the cash register by the door and a boy stood behind the counter. The boy held out his hand for the prescription and, glancing at it, asked if it was for a child. Reassured, I waited. A minute or two later, the boy returned and plonked down on the counter a large box labelled Spasmocibalgine Suppositories. In some alarm I looked at the prescription: it read Benadryl Elixir. I protested to the man at the cash register. He shrugged his shoulders. 'He is only a boy,' he said.

Eventually the Station Commander intervened: he could not have an officer spending half his day driving up and down, it interfered with his work. Work was the magic word. The air-conditioner was approved and thenceforth all five of us slept in the same room. My daughter's health stabilised and, as the doctor had hopefully predicted, 'she grew out of it'.

Our Beirut life was brought to a sudden end. Just after New Year 1967 a telegram from Head Office arrived informing me that I was cross-posted to Benghazi as Head of Station and that I was to take up the appointment in seventeen days' time. No explanation for the urgency was given. I was required to travel via London where, I assumed, all would be made clear. My successor arrived and a hurried handover of my agents followed. I set in motion arrangements at the Embassy for the transfer of the family but had to leave the pack-up to my wife. I left for London with four days to spare.

Benghazi

As I sat on the plane my thoughts turned to what lay ahead. I was of course very pleased to be given command of a station, albeit a sub-station; it was a step forward in my career. Benghazi was a surprise: who ever would have thought of being posted there? I knew of Benghazi from the war when as a twelve-year-old I followed the North Africa campaign with Rommel, the Desert Fox, chasing and being chased in turn by the Desert Rats along the coast, the siege of Tobruk, Alamein and all that. What of Benghazi in 1967? Evidently, it was no backwater.

I reported to the desk officer for Libya. The reason for haste, he explained, was administrative. Personnel had to bring forward planned postings because of the personal problems of one of those involved. As to the tasks of the station the principal one, indeed the reason for its existence, was to monitor the stability of the regime and in particular the threat of Egyptian-inspired subversion. The station had liaison relationships with the local security service, the British Army and CIA and, as always, looked out for Russian intelligence activity.

Turning to the relationship between the two stations, the desk officer said that was for discussion with H/Tripoli during my stop-over on the way to Benghazi. All he said about the man himself was that he had served in the military (Highland Brigade), spoke Arabic (ex-Sudan Political Service) and had an authoritative manner. Forewarned, I went on my way and was met at the airport by the station secretary and delivered to H/Tripoli's villa. There was Scottish in his voice and he affected the air of a laird talking to his estate manager, pipe in one hand, a glass in the other. I raised the question of the inter-relationship of the stations and my standing was made clear. On parting, he expressed the hope that I would do better than the man I was replacing.

In contrast, H/Benghazi's welcome was warm and positive. There was a lot to pack into the few days of the handover, including the each-way drive of 200 kms to the liaison service headquarters at Bayda, in the heart of the Jebel Akhdar, the Green Mountain. The days passed in a blur. It was piercingly cold, there seemed to be no heating anywhere. At the final event, a before-lunch drinks with the majors of the British Army Training Team, I shivered, lost in the noisy bonhomie, with a glass of Bull's Blood, a mixture of beef consommé, vodka and ice, rattling in my hand.

The ordeal was over and I became H/Benghazi, a First Secretary in the Consulate-General which was in effect a mini-Embassy with a full range of functions. It was housed in three adjacent buildings dating from the Italian colonial period one of which, the Consul-General's office, was fortified. Across the road stood Mosquito House, his residence, a villa with walls and garden. The whole formed a little enclave in which all but three of the staff lived and worked. I was one of those who lived elsewhere.

The station occupied a single room which I shared with the station secretary and her dog, a small undistinguished animal by the name of Mrs Brown. A large safe contained the station's papers and it was to these that I turned to consolidate what little grip I had on my responsibilities. All that was fixed up was a meeting some days ahead with a British academic at the university who was our window on student attitudes and activities.

Having met the Army majors during the handover, I thought to make a start by calling on their commanding officer. He had his headquarters in D'Aosta Barracks, the erstwhile Italian Army HQ in Cyrenaica, and had oversight of the extensive British military presence in Libya. In addition to the Training Team, it consisted of a battalion of the Inniskilling Dragoon Guards in Wavell Barracks on the outskirts of Benghazi, an office in Tobruk for liaison with the Palace and El Adem airfield and the desert training base. The Colonel was genial and unpretentious, at ease in his command. In his last appointment, he enjoyed, even encouraged, perceptions of him as a blimpish figure.

My family arrived and were somewhat taken aback by their new home which had none of the elegance of the Beirut house; it was a bungalow on a concrete plinth in a flood area over which pi dogs roamed. Similar bungalows were dotted around at random; there were no marked roads, so no addresses. The flood, an annual event, was the run-off from the Jebel Akhdar following the spring rains. The water arrived silently and crept up inch by inch to form a placid blue lake on which the bungalows appeared to float.

We took on my predecessor's cook/houseboy, Umran, an unimaginative cook with a smile that exposed alarming orange teeth. Schooled in the practices of the Army canteen, he invariably set the table with bottles of tomato and HP sauce. We also kept on the obligatory but unnecessary night-watchman who came at dusk to be paid for sleeping away from home. We were undisturbed due perhaps to the dogs, large dusty yellow animals, which the locals needlessly feared. Only the 'eggis' boy, a local lad selling small eggs which he carried in a paint tin, was undeterred. One day, he proudly offered us 'inglizi eggis', large eggs bearing a lion stamp which, to his bafflement, we refused.

We settled into our new simpler life, the sophistication and amenities of Beirut soon forgotten. In town, there was only one recognisably European-style shop selling women's clothes and a single restaurant known as the Greasy Spoon. The children went to the British Council school and my wife became one of the teachers. We had use of the Officers' Beach Club with its simple restaurant and could shop at the NAAFI in Wavell Barracks. We generally lived under the Army's umbrella, detached from the local population. At weekends we visited Cyrene, the ancient Greek capital of Cyrenaica, on the Jebel Akhdar or picnicked in the scrubby desert, awash in spring with the purple-red of wild gladioli. It was like living in a former colony we had not left on independence. And so it seemed to the local population, as we were to find out.

Control of security in Cyrenaica was exercised by the Cyrenaica Defence Force (CYDEF) which had evolved from the force formed during the war to support the military campaign. I visited the headquarters in Bayda every two or three weeks to keep myself before their eyes but such visits were superficial, of a courtesy nature. I needed to get to grips with liaison close at hand and called on the Aqeed, the Colonel, in command in Benghazi. I declared my role to him and offered Service support for his efforts to combat subversion and, by means of an exaggerated description of the Russian threat, obtained his permission to talk directly to Special Branch.

The Special Branch office, when I eventually found it, was a portacabin in the dunes. It was a cold raw day and I found its two occupants hunched in their overcoats over an electric fire turned on its side. On it, a teapot bubbled, boiling the tea that turns teeth orange. The younger officer spoke English, his grey-haired superior did not. I toiled through my presentation and at the end said that I was ready to help in any way I could. When translated, this produced a reaction from the older man who thus far had only grunted. An argument between the two followed, at the end of which the young officer, embarrassed, said 'The Colonel thanks for very much and asks you to get him a carpet from the NAAFI'.

Colonel Martin invited me to accompany him on a visit to the El Adem training base in the desert beyond Tobruk. We broke the six-hour journey at a CYDEF Regional HQ where a guard of honour shuffled into line as we drove into the compound. In the Commander's office, we were served a version of inglizi tea made with condensed milk and very sweet. The Brigadier, looking at me, patted Colonel Martin's knee and said 'Colonel Martin…good man.' Colonel Martin, in turn, patted the Brigadier's knee and, turning to me, said 'Brigadier Ahmed…good man.' After a pause, the performance was repeated. Seemingly unsubstantial, there was a lesson to be learned from these courtesies.

The purpose of the Colonel's visit to El Adem was to give a decision on the request for additional funds for the removal of night-soil. The local Bedouin who performed this task had put up their prices and in response, the Base had attempted to dig latrine pits with discouraging results. We sat solemnly through the Base Commander's presentation, then went out to inspect a hole the size of a manhole-cover six inches deep hewn out of solid rock. As Col Martin later observed, it was not the British Army's finest hour.

I made progress on the student target. At the planned meeting with the British academic he told me that he would soon be leaving, which my predecessor had not mentioned. My heart sank then rose a little as he continued that he would try to get one of his students to agree to meet me. The student did agree and when I went to the address given, the students' lodging, I found not one but three of them there. They lost no time in attacking me over the Balfour Declaration and Britain's support for Israel but the storm blew itself out and we talked about their lives and what I thought about their country. Late in the evening, after a plate of macaroni and lamb that had been slowly cooking, we broke up and agreed to meet again.

So, the Kitchen Club, as we called it, came into being and we met at intervals throughout my time in Benghazi. I even spent a night under canvas with them. They were perfectly aware that I was an intelligence officer but never asked me just as I never asked them why they were prepared to talk to me under clandestine arrangements. We were in a conscious bubble, in today's language, a private chat-room. They assured me that there was no Egyptian meddling at University. There was no need of it, Radio Cairo took care of that.

During May, tensions rose between Israel and its neighbours and at the beginning of June we were instructed by HO to destroy our records and prepare for disorder. The emergency equipment we had on the station was an incendiary deedbox and the emergency radio set of WWII vintage that was standard issue to all stations. In the incendiary deedbox I placed the sole record I had retained, the irrecoverable station account of expenditure for the month. I could not decide what to do about the radio. The instructions were that it should be cached in some secure location from which it could be recovered when conditions permitted. I could not think where this might be in our circumstances and kept the radio in the office.

Groups of men started to form at the end of the road. The Aqeed reassured me: there was no cause for alarm, everything was under control. The tribes knew that the King loved Britain and would see that we came to no harm. Who then were these people hanging around the Consulate? They are just some troublemakers: ignore them.

On June 6th, the Six Day War started. By mid-morning, a crowd of several hundred surged round the Consulate chanting and, urged on by a ring-leader, started throwing stones at the windows. The front door came under attack. The Consul-General, a trickle of blood on his cheek from flying glass, called the Army to the rescue. With the assurance of rescue, the staff remained calm, quietly shredding remaining papers and destroying the Consulate's cypher machine as instructed by London. The Army was unaccountably slow. The front door showed signs of giving way.

At last, the Army arrived and the crowd fell back, silent, and watched as we walked out. We were taken to D'Aosta Barracks. Meanwhile, the children from school had assembled in Mosquito House and, in the course of the day, they and all the Consulate staff and families, including my secretary's visiting aunt, were reunited in D'Aosta Barracks. Towards midnight the Army rescued the beleaguered American Consulate staff who were trapped in their strong room, unable to open the door owing to damage to the lock by rioters. They eventually squeezed out through the small window in the strongroom after the protecting grille had been pulled out by the Army. When the full picture became clear, every building in Benghazi associated with Britain and America had been attacked. The Libyan flag had been raised over the American Consulate. In Tripoli, there were demonstrations but no violence.

On arrival at the barracks, I was impatient to be the first to break the news. With my emergency radio set I was the only member of the Consulate with communications. We draped the aerial over a door and the DWS man tapped the message that all staff were safe and sound. I was told later it was the first time that the radio had ever been used for its intended purpose and, at a guess, it was also the last croak of the dodo. Full communications were restored using military channels.

In the barracks we lived on top of each other, families sharing the same room. For the children it was quite an adventure. They played with the tortoises that curiously abounded in the barracks and were perfectly happy with the monotonous diet of fish fingers and tinned peaches. The tannoy was in continuous operation broadcasting news and music. One evening after the end of the war, I was leaning over the rail outside our room looking down on the partly lit parade ground when on the still, hot night air came the voice of Nasser. He spoke slowly as if the words had to be dragged out, his voice heavy with sadness and defeat. I was spellbound and felt the shame of the Arabs. When we went home, we found that all our clothes had been taken along with the sewing machine and radio, but the house had not been disturbed. By chance I had a suit at the cleaners.

In the aftermath, the Libyan Government, alarmed by the violent public reaction, requested the withdrawal of the British military presence. Perversely, relations between the two countries became closer from which I benefitted, as the Aqeed, now shocked out of complacency, was worried about subversion and wanted to do something about it. He asked for help with training a group of young officers. Unfortunately, he had got it into his head that the threat came from the KGB and was unshakeable in his belief that knowledge of Russian by his officers was essential.

HO reacted with consternation to the request to find an Arabic-speaking teacher of Russian. I managed to restrain the Aqeed, who was talking about the need also for Polish and Czech, explaining the difficulty of finding teachers and persuaded him that the best course was to bring the students' English up to scratch as the first step. On this basis we went ahead. A day or two before New Year, the Aqeed's deputy came to the Consulate with a box of money for me to look after to avoid having to return it as unspent funds. The amount was not stated and no receipt required. After the officer left I counted the equivalent of over £70,000.

The Aqeed was invited to London and fêted appropriately. I was on hand to steer him through the meetings, after one of which the Libya desk officer praised the brilliant way I had handled a tricky question. 'Oh,' said I, 'how was that?' 'You ignored it', he said, 'you didn't reply.' I had not heard the question. I took the Aqeed to the Post Office Tower with its revolving restaurant, always a useful topic to fall back on when conversation flagged. The menu was pretentious with lists of dishes in French. We worked through them with the waiter without progress. The Aqeed took charge: Do you have fish? Yes. Fried fish? Yes. Do you have chips? Yes.

The highlight of the visit was the revelation that the Controller, the area director, had served in CYDEF during the war. Could this be true? The Aqeed expressed delight but, suspicious tribesman that he was, later asked me to write down the Controller's name for him. He was going to check. It was indeed true; the Controller had served with the 1st Battalion. A full programme was laid on for a visit by him to Benghazi which began with a lunch of welcome, a cold buffet. Pointing to a bowl of diced vegetables in mayonnaise, the Aqeed asked me what it was called. Russian Salad. He called a waiter over and told him to remove the dish. Turning to me he said with a smile, 'We don't want anything Russian.'

With a CYDEF escort we drove up to Bayda, stopping for refreshments on the way at a station where a guard of honour of supposedly 1st Battalion veterans awaited the Controller's inspection.

At HQ we were shown the roll of men who had served during the war, the General himself pointing to his listing as a Sergeant, the most senior rank attained by a Libyan. My Aqeed had been a Lance-Corporal. On return to Benghazi we visited the abandoned war-time barracks. The visit was a great success. The comradeship of the war, despite all that had changed, still had resonance.

For all the good will and sweet talk, I had not managed to get any real support from liaison for my efforts against the Russian target and instead had sent the Aqeed haring off in the wrong direction. There was one identified KGB officer in Benghazi. He did not hide himself away and had struck up a connection with the British golfers in Benghazi. Now and then he presented himself at the caravan in the dunes where the golfers met to socialise. They enjoyed the company of Ivan the Terrible, as they called him after his first name, and he let himself go in the boisterous Russian way. At a Christmas gathering, with a mince pie in his hand, he went around saying 'who is spy?'. That was about all we knew, except that he once urinated on the side of the caravan, this from the golfer who urinated alongside. For some reason, opaque to me, HO found this of particular interest. Or was their interest engaged by the mince spy episode?

Meanwhile, the withdrawal of the military got underway and the Ministry of Foreign Affairs posted a small liaison team to Benghazi. At a gathering to welcome the team, I got talking to a thirty-year-old very pleased with his excellent English and cosmopolitan outlook. As an Intelligence Officer Never Sleeps, I chatted him up to see where it might go. I gave him lunch and in return we were invited, the whole family, to lunch to meet his wife and children. In the course of the meal, my elder daughter whispered to me that she wanted to go to the lavatory. With sweet understanding smiles, the wife of the official led her away. Back at the table my daughter whispered audibly, 'Daddy, they've got dirty lavatories.'

I saw him again a couple of times, finding him increasingly hard work as he was so serious-minded. In general conversation, I talked about Cyrene which prompted him to say without a trace of humour,

'For Englishman, Libya is very good: there are many ruins. For Libyan man, London is very good: there are many nightclubs.' I took this to be a joke and laughed but he had said it so solemnly that I wondered if it was his considered opinion.

My CIA colleague was a kindred spirit. He was of my age and like me in his first command. He was the first CIA officer I had to deal with and my secretary described how we circled round each other at the first meeting in my office. He too was under the supervision of Tripoli and I got to know his boss who quite often came to Benghazi. On one occasion he described his frustration with H/Tripoli who, he said, had pulled down the tartan curtain.

Mid-tour leave was coming up. In view of the changed political climate following the disturbances, I asked HO if I would be returning to Benghazi. Libya had a new pro-British Prime Minister, on whom I myself had called, and relations with the liaison could hardly be better, though frustratingly lacking in substance. The Aqeed had been placed in overall charge of security and was now in Tripoli beyond my reach. There were dissidents, as the disturbances had shown, and it was to be hoped that that CYDEF, alerted to threat, would be energetic in dealing with them. HO did not respond. On the eve of our departure, I sent a telegram saying that I was proceeding on leave on the assumption that we would return to Benghazi.

Tripoli

Summer 1968. Towards the end of our leave I telephoned the Office to find out if they had come to a decision about Benghazi. They had, the station was to close and I was to take over from H/Tripoli. I was of course gratified by this advancement and the job held no fears, but the prospect of the handover filled me with foreboding. We had not formed the usual comradely relationship and, knowing his character, I was sure he would resent being replaced by his subordinate. I was in for a difficult time.

New appointment, new car. This time I chose an Austin Cambridge, a rather ponderous estate car with heavy steering and ungainly in manoeuvre. We drove in three stages to Naples, from where we would go by sea to Tripoli. With two days in hand, we decided not to stay in Naples and went on to Sorrento in the hope of experiencing its come-back-to allure. Disappointingly, we had go-away weather and it was a relief to board the warm and dry Citta di Livorno. The boat had a permanent list to port, the result, we were told, of having been sunk twice during the war. The effect only made itself felt in the cabin. If you had the bunk on the starboard side you risked falling out of bed when you turned over, and on the port side of being unable to turn over.

On arrival, we were taken to the house chosen for us by the departing H/Tripoli. It was in stark contrast to his own which he had taken over from his predecessor, a villa on the sea-shore in Giorgimpopoli, the fashionable residential area of Tripoli. He had argued on security principles that a third H/Tripoli should live elsewhere and HO agreed. Thus we found ourselves in a semi-detached house on a slip-road below a supermarket on a busy main road. Our neighbour on the open side kept a sheep for Ramadhan in the small dusty forecourt. It took months to extricate ourselves and move to a more suitable house on the outskirts of Tripoli.

The handover proved as ungenerous as I feared. H/Tripoli presented me to his few contacts as the economy version of himself and even failed to introduce one of them on the grounds that the contact was too upset by his departure. However, the handovers to the two liaison contacts were sabotage-proof. Indeed, with the local liaison I had the higher ground as my friend, the Aqeed, was now in Tripoli in overall charge. I met the new CIA station chief over a drink at H/Tripoli's house. Attempting to peep round the Tartan Curtain, he asked H/Tripoli, a self-professed connoisseur of whisky, for advice on what to buy. Puffing on his pipe, H/Tripoli drawled that the only whisky he could recommend was made by a small distillery in Islay for selected customers. A close observer of him as he poured our whiskies would have spotted that he poured his own from a different bottle.

With the change of command, the station brief had been given a tweak to take account of the now benign political climate. I was not to 'follow down the well-worn paths of Chancery' but to concentrate on Soviet Bloc work exploiting the good relations with liaison. An Arabic-speaking probationer would be posted to the Station to 'get among the young Turks'. How easy it all sounds sitting at a desk in HO. I was also to visit Tunis at intervals to maintain the link with the Tunisian Security Service. This sounded attractive. As soon as I was settled in, I promised myself a visit to Tunis.

The settling-in process was laborious. In our dusty urban setting we missed the simpler, open life of Benghazi. There was no flood water in Tripoli. It was an Italian city with a cathedral, Italian grocers and restaurants, horse-drawn gharries on the corniche and a bust of Scipio Africanus in the market square. However it lacked the vibrancy of an Italian city and seemed to us newcomers rather characterless. With its amenities and sophistication, more apparent than real, and with its government buildings, banks, and embassies, we felt returned to conventional nine-to-five life in contrast to free-style gritty Benghazi.

My elder daughter had started at boarding school in the UK. The other two children went to the British Council school and came home chanting 'watani watani watani', the opening words of the Libyan national anthem, which they had been taught, presumably in a spirit of ecumenism. We bought a small over-sexed poodle which was plagued by the ticks from next door's sheep. We played crazy golf on the championship course in Tripoli, one of the holes of which was halfway up a wall. We picnicked at the beach and visited the ancient cities of Sabratha and Leptis Magna. In short, we made a family life for ourselves.

As I promised myself, I visited Tunis. I was received by the Director-General, urbane, confident, very French. We quickly fell into an easy conversation which ranged far beyond the security concerns of Tunisia. With a mental sigh, I contrasted him to my Aqeed. The Ambassador invited me for lunch and at the end of the morning I went with him to his residence. During the drive, conversation died away as the Ambassador became increasingly preoccupied and on arrival he waved me on into the house. He came in a few minutes later apologising for the smell of onions in the car. Investigating, he had found a sack of onions in the boot, despite having reprimanded the driver a week earlier after finding a live goat in the boot.

His wife soothed him. He poured two glasses of sherry in those small-waisted glasses ('You don't want one, do you, darling') with the concentration of a dispensing chemist. In their last post before retirement ambassadors are notoriously stingy. He had the grey look of a First World War general, his bristly moustache brushed forward up his nose. On learning that my first posting had been to Athens, he reminisced about his own first posting also to Athens as Third Secretary at the time of the restoration of the Greek monarchy in 1935. He recalled that George Beta had no proper household to start with and used to send down to the Residence to borrow the Ambassador's cutlery when entertaining. A voice from the past. Having dealt with all official business on the first day of my visit, I had the second to spend in Tunis, a magical Arab city with its 8th century mosque and medieval arcaded souk. A must for the family to see.

Six months later during the Easter school holidays we set off by road for Tunis, an 800 mile journey. A ghibli, the strong hot sand-laden wind from the Sahara, was blowing. In the yellow fog visibility was thirty yards or less. After three hours we were over the border and pulled in at a roadside café for something to eat. Silence fell as we walked in. The group of men in the café turned to watch us and continued to watch us in silence as if we were a performing troupe of Martians. Hoping for the best, we had the soup of the day in which the pieces of white floating in it turned out not to be pasta but tripe. We spent the first night at the resort of Djerba and in the ensuing days visited the 7th century mosque at Kairouan, and ancient Carthage, which had been so effectively destroyed by Rome as to leave no ruins. In Tunis we stayed in the old quarter and feasted on anchovies and lamb couscous.

Meanwhile in Tripoli a storm had brewed up. As part of an aid project a team of young nurses and technicians from the NHS arrived in a fanfare of publicity to support the Tripoli hospital. They were accommodated in a hotel and, when attention to them fell away, they were left to their own devices. The Vice Police pounced and arrested a couple found to be in a state of undress and charged them with immorality. The nurses felt terrorised and the Embassy protested. At the Ambassador's request I went to see the Chief of Police, whom I had first met on the 'well-worn paths of Chancery' on which he walked comfortably with his excellent English and urbane manner. I appealed to him as a man of the world. He would know that, whatever the truth of the matter, couples did behave in such ways and in the wider interests of the project the charges should be dropped. He said that he would see to it, adding, 'The people here are very ignorant, they do not understand that the English girl cannot sleep alone'.

Far more serious was the growing and increasingly vocal criticism within the Libyan Army of the proposed BAC missile deal and of senior officers accused of supporting it for personal gain. The focus of attack was Col Abdul Aziz Shelhi, a controversial figure untouchable because of the King's favour which he enjoyed as the son of a former courtier close to the King. I asked the Aqeed if he was concerned. Whatever he felt, he took the party line. The concern was exaggerated and in any case was out of his hands: it was for the Army to deal with it, the Army would not tolerate any intervention by him. That was certainly true.

In the hope of bringing the situation under control, a senior British general was brought in to conduct a review of the requirement for missiles. General Mogg went diligently about his task. He visited units spruced up for the occasion and tales circulated about his suppressed rage at finding sighting and ranging instruments painted over. Predictably, he found the requirement valid and the Libyan government approved the deal. BAC drew up an extensive training programme with courses starting in August 1969. Two trainees failed to turn up for reasons which later became apparent.

In mid-August, I was invited to Army Headquarters by Colonels Aun Rahuma and Abdul Aziz Shalhi, the third and fourth ranking officers in the Army. They asked if the Service could advise on setting up a security unit in the Army. I replied that it could certainly be considered but it had political implications. I went on to ask if there were security concerns. No, no, no, all officers were loyal to His Majesty. On that note the meeting ended. Decisive action was required, not a security unit to hide behind. The Government was nervous and relays of envoys visited Turkey, where the King was on holiday, to persuade him to return.

1st September 1969, 6am, the phone rang. It was the Head of Chancery: 'You had better come in. Something is happening, there are soldiers around.' My wife and daughters were in England. I woke the au pair and left for the office. I drove through deserted streets to the central area where I was stopped by an armed soldier. In Arabic, he asked where I was going. To the British Embassy. There is no Embassy, he said with a gesture of dismissal. I was in sight of the Information Officer's flat. Pointing to it, I said that it was my house and the soldier waved me on.

I found the 'young turk' probationer at the flat and, with him following the Arabic, the three of us spent the day listening to the radio. Continuous martial music was interrupted at intervals by announcements of support for the revolution notionally from towns around the country and declarations by the Brothers of the Revolutionary Command Council, including one announcing the promotion of Lt Muammar Qadhafi to the rank of Captain in recognition of his services to the revolution. Who was this Qadhafi? Around midnight, the Head of Chancery as Acting Head of Mission was picked up with his Western counterparts by armoured car and taken to Army HQ to receive from Qadhafi the formal declaration of the assumption of power. The escorting officer was in high spirits and quoted from Churchill's speeches during the journey.

The following day we moved in with the Head of Chancery, as he proposed, because of the isolated position of our house. Thus, with the au pair, my son, aged eight, and Sammy the poodle, we joined a household which included the daughter aged five, a dachshund called Otto and a grey parrot. On return from the office at lunchtime, I asked the girl if Sammy had been good. Oh yes, she said, he's been playing piggybacks with Otto all morning.

During our stay, the parrot escaped and fluttered into the garden of the neighbour who happened to be the Black Prince, a shadowy member of the royal family. Revolution or no revolution, Mrs Head of Chancery went round, rang the doorbell and explained to the staff, boggling with incredulity, that she had come about the parrot. We returned home after two or three days to find a banner headline in Arabic painted on the surrounding wall: 'This is the house of Aun

Rahuma murderer of Idris Aissawi patriot'. Passers-by threw stones over the wall.

Soldiers were placed on guard round the Embassy and two or three surveillance cars stood ready across the road to follow all who left by car. An armed squad entered the building looking for 'radio sets for talking to Israel' and refused at first to leave. A dusk to dawn curfew was in force with permits only for the Consul and Head of Mission. The street names and directions in Italian disappeared, transforming Tripoli as if by magic into an Arab city.

The Brothers of the Revolutionary Command Council showed themselves to the people; all young officers of the rank of Captain except for Qadhafi, a little older, and one Lieutenant Colonel. On black and white television we watched a lorry moving slowly through the crowd in Market Square, on the open back of which stood Qadhafi, already sporting a slightly too large cap, waving to the crowd. Having reached the dais, surrounded by the Brothers, he began an interminable speech consisting of the repetition of a few phrases, such as 'The glorious people of Libya'. He was no orator. In Benghazi, led by Qadhafi, the Brothers strode into the stadium like a triumphant football team to receive the acclamation of the crowd, handsome young men excited by their success. Not a shot fired. No resistance. The new leaders, a new dawn.

We received a stream of telegrams from a seemingly uncomprehending HO, asking questions to which we had no useful answer. I was asked when I had last seen the Aqeed and replied unhelpfully that it was on television when being marched off into detention with other senior officers. It seemed that a counter-coup was under consideration, as one telegram asked where on the coast a party might land and find the local people supportive. In reply, I asked in whose name would this intervention be made. The plain fact was that the King, for all the respect of his status and historical role, had lost potency and the traditional support of the tribes had become a myth. Restore the regime to reinstate Abdul Aziz Shelhi?

A new dawn but no new government. In the vacuum, grumbling

started about the curfew, the closure of the airport, delays at the port, shelves emptying in the shops. The Embassy scratched around for information from British residents who came to register with the Consul. One British businessman became so frequent a visitor to the Embassy that he was deported. An officer of the CIA station, frustrated beyond endurance by the surveillance, took to letting down the tyres of the cars waiting outside his house as the surveillants sat in them.

As days turned into weeks, a semblance of normality returned. Ministers were appointed among whom I was proud to see one of my boys from the Kitchen Club, while another of them was appointed to an administrative function at the university. An Algerian working for an American oil company, who had written to Qadhafi telling him what needed to be done, found himself appointed Prime Minister. Putting two and two together, we worked out that the timing of the coup had been determined by the BAC courses which would split up the plotters. It was also evident that Qadhafi must have been well known to the Army command as a troublemaker because of his failure to progress to Captain, unheard of in an Arab Army, which in turn explained the announcement of his promotion in the first hours of the coup. Qadhafi promoted himself to Colonel but no higher, it was believed, out of reverence of Col Nasser, his inspiration.

Our new Ambassador arrived: Donald Maitland, small of stature but with a large, confident personality. I found him to have a taste for irony and satire which brought us together and I enjoyed a freer relationship with him, because not in the line of command, than he had with his own staff. I was with him when his telephone call to Benghazi came through for his first conversation with the Consul-General. Before picking up the phone, he went through a stress-relieving routine and I saw how tightly wound he was. I sat with him before his first meeting with Qadhafi. Visualising the scene, he rehearsed what he would say, perhaps a little joke here and a personal note there. The eventual meeting, essentially a protocol occasion, went well in his estimation, the array of guns on the table pointing towards him providing material for a little joke. A former Director of MECAS, the Ambassador took pride in his Arabic.

All well and good, but the trouble was that the Ambassador came with the pre-formed belief that Britain had a 'white history' having liberated Libya from Italian rule and stewarded her to nationhood, and that this would provide the basis for a good future relationship. I felt that this was over-optimistic and did not take into account the recalcitrant character of the Libyan people or the nature of the revolution. Nevertheless, the 'white history' theory became the policy of the Embassy and the climax was to be the ceremonial handover of the keys of British property. These were the keys to the Anglican church in Tripoli and to the villa built for Graziani, Mussolini's Army commander, near Cyrene, which the King gave to Britain after the war. A meeting with Qadhafi was requested and agreed, time and place to be advised. The hours dragged by but at last the call came at 9pm. An escort conducted the Ambassador to an empty government building in darkness and to a cold room in which an officer, working overtime, sat in his greatcoat. The Ambassador explained his purpose. 'Give the keys to me,' said the officer. And that was that.

The Welfare Section of the FCO sent a few films by bag to keep our spirits up. One of the films was the glorious 'Carry On Up the Khyber' with Private Widdle and the Khazi of Calabar. It was shown in the Embassy basement with chairs arranged in rows. By themselves in the front row, the Ambassador sat with his reserved and distant wife. Both sat ramrod straight throughout the film. I knew the Ambassador would have enjoyed it, deploring perhaps the most brazen vulgarity, but was constrained by his wife. It was a scene and a setting that could have been in the film itself.

The Consul was not one of the gilded elite and had reached his position by years of toil. A close reader of the regulations, he performed the role of shop steward. At the morning meeting he raised the question of the availability of the pool at the Residence which, according to regulations, was not for the sole use of the Ambassador and was available to staff. The Ambassador waved his hand in acquiescence. My daughters and I made full use of this amenity, usually having the pool to ourselves in the late afternoon. On two occasions we met guests of the Ambassador taking a dip. One was Lord Lichfield, the photographer. Sitting beside him, feet dangling in the pool, he offered to put me up for the Alpine Club even though my experience of the Alps was limited to the school visit. The other bather was the Bishop of Cape Town, visiting the farthest flung parish of his province. When it became chilly he went in to change, followed soon after by me. I found him naked, mopping his large pink body with a handkerchief.

I had to get my own show back on the road. As a declared officer, I was now a sitting duck for the new security service. A car swung in behind me whenever I left the office and parked opposite the house. I observed that the surveillants withdrew after a time without evident replacement. I tested this; it seemed that after dark I was off the hook, for what it was worth. I had no agents and, not having gone down the well-worn paths of Chancery, no contacts in the British community. The Libyans I knew were in prison. HO told me that the top priority was now to develop agents with access to the Revolutionary Command Council. Some hope.

The only potential assets I had were the two Kitchen Club members who had joined the cause. The one who was now a minister was an unworldly idealist and in any case quite out of reach. The other had more of an agent feel about him and was in a less exposed position in his appointment at the university. The probationer had established a conscious contact with a young English teacher at the university in his search for access to Young Turks. Could the teacher act as a go-between to set up a meeting? It was worth a try.

SovBloc work was in the doldrums. I got alongside, in the time-honoured phrase, a Czech architect working in some advisory capacity who had been stranded by the revolution. He knew perfectly well what I was up to and was happy to add a dimension to his life. Professionally, nothing of moment came from the relationship which we both enjoyed, especially the heavy irony of the long political jokes he was fond of telling.

I flew to Rome to compare notes with Italian liaison and to see if they had any resources. I stopped over in Malta to talk about the interest Qadhafi was showing in the island's historic Islamic connections. I went to Tunis where liaison fell on me with a thousand questions, one repeated over and over: 'How could you have allowed this to happen.' A different Director-General was in charge. I enquired after his predecessor. He was in prison: did you wish to see him? I declined, saying that I thought it inappropriate. He assured me that it would not be regarded as such: I could see him, 'à titre d'amitié,' as a friend. As a parting gift, I was given a bottle of liqueur that tasted like cough mixture and a bottle of Tunisian champagne, which ended up on the bottle stall at the school's fete.

I was yesterday's man and my days surely numbered. What the Service needed was an undeclared officer with a cover job in the Embassy to give him some projection. Suddenly Donald Maitland was recalled, at Edward Heath's request, to become his press secretary at No 10. He left within days, ignoring the usual diplomatic courtesies, glad to get away. The 'white history' had turned out to be a grey history, and the plan had not been the success he hoped.

Conscious that time was slipping away, my remaining objective was to make contact with my Kitchen Club protégé for the pleasure of seeing him again, but more for the professional satisfaction of seeing him clandestinely as an agent, if only once, to bring to a close my venture with the Kitchen Club. Through the probationer's contact the RV was arranged.

Feeling very exposed, I waited in the dark at the pick-up point in a part of Tripoli I did not know. A car stopped. I got into the back and crouched down in the well as instructed. After a few minutes, the car turned off the tarmac and drove more slowly along bumpy unmade roads. The car stopped and, to my alarm, I heard the driver talking to someone. After the exchange of conversation we drove on to his house. We talked for two hours or more, partly catch-up and partly about his experience as a volunteer in the service of the revolution. As expected, I did not learn anything of significant value but there was enough for an intelligence report with all the trimmings.

A date in June 1970 was set for our departure. In the supermarket, I spotted the head of the KGB station wandering around amid the jars of Bulgarian pickled cucumbers and other East European produce on the mostly empty shelves. Though we had never spoken we knew each other. I went over to him and told him I was leaving. He held out his hand and said, 'Congratulations'.

Immersion in Africa

We had been away for six years during which time we had given no thought to the family home. It was in the hands of a letting agency who had not troubled us with decisions. Fully realising that our long absence would have taken its toll, we nevertheless opened the front door with pleasurable anticipation but our hopes came crashing down. The scene was one of grime and neglect. One corner of the hall ceiling had come down. The dining room had clearly been used as a bedsitter and, as we went from room to room, the fat stains on the walls suggested that the tenant had sublet them. The letting agent denied knowing of any irregularity and brushed aside our complaints: the rent had continued to come in.

Depressed by the scale of the restoration work, we decided we had to move. As both girls were at school in Oxford, we made exploratory visits to the area. We looked at a cottagey house in a village to the west of Oxford and, to the east, a dull house on the outskirts of Aylesbury. Neither made the heart leap and the daily commute was unthinkable. Living in our dingy house breathed life back into it and we gave up thought of moving. I decided to tackle the kitchen first. So began six years of DIY and gardening.

I reported for duty at the Tower of Light, as we called the unlovely tower block near Lambeth North tube, to learn what was in store for me. My new job was to be the desk officer for Southern Africa, Daphne's old job. I then learned that I would be taking over from my predecessor in Tripoli. The Personnel Officer calmed me down saying that there would be no handover as he was away in Northern Ireland liaising with the Army. We talked about Tripoli and, as a by-the-way, he mentioned that the Controller had given me a bad report for lack of effort. What! What! I spluttered.

Back to my old parish, it was familiar territory. I had four stations to look after, three of which worked on differing aspects of the Rhodesia target. This had to be done from outside Rhodesia, which had become a no-go area following the Unilateral Declaration of Independence (UDI) in 1965. The fourth station was Kinshasa where Daphne's successors strove to cling on in the shifting political environment. All four were as usual required to study Soviet bloc activity. I had at my side, in my former role, an assistant desk officer, a secretary and an R for Requirements desk officer who processed reports from the stations, liaised with the Foreign Office, and attended Whitehall assessment meetings.

One of my early tasks was to deal with a stay-behind agent returning from Rhodesia. He was one of a number who, at the time of UDI, agreed to remain in place in the face of the Government's call for members of the British community to leave or lose their pension rights. He had come to claim his pension rights as promised. As procedure required, I saw him under cover of an alias, an exaggerated precaution in the circumstances. For amusement and in the hope of provoking a reaction from the Controller for Africa, a very particular man, I picked the name Clamp from the available list and, as Ron Clamp, I met the agent in Moon's Temperance Billiard Rooms under Victoria Coach Station, a suitable low-life venue. As I hoped, C/Africa called me to his office and, with the contact note in his hand, said in his testy, donnish way, 'Couldn't you have chosen a less plebeian name?'

When I had settled in, I went to see the stations working on the Rhodesia targets, starting with Lusaka. I arrived at 4am and, in the absence of instructions, assumed that I would be met and so did not take the bus to the InterContinental Hotel with all the other passengers. As a result, I spent three hours alone in the darkened airport before staff came on duty and I could make a start on getting myself rescued.

The drive to the office failed to rekindle any excitement at being in the heart of Africa. There was nothing exotic about Lusaka. The day wore on meeting, greeting, and talking and I was glad to be spared entertainment on my first evening. I had dinner at the hotel and asked the waiter what was the national dish. Steak and chips, he said. I eventually wormed out of him that Zambians ate something called nshima, which I hoped would be a local speciality but found it to be a tasteless white stodge made from maize. While eating it, I glanced at the local newspaper. A lot of space was given to the indignation and complaints of a man on finding out that Lemon, his newly-wed wife, was a man.

I had arranged my trip to include Sunday in Lusaka and, as hoped, I was taken to a reserve, a lake, to watch birds. Though described as nearby, to get there and back was a long bone-shaking drive on rutted roads either slowly or at break-neck speed in theory to fly over the ruts. The lake was a featureless grey expanse under the overcast sky. We sat in the humid heat, binoculars at the ready to catch a flutter but all we could study at our leisure were two lugubrious Malibu storks. However, this was more like Africa, the wide sky and far horizon, the heat and the dust.

Much of the station's effort was devoted, in our parlance, to 'getting among' the freedom fighter organisations active in Lusaka, ZANU and ZAPU (Rhodesia), ANC (South Africa) and FRELIMO (Mozambique). Of principal interest were ZANU and ZAPU and contacts were developed, despite initial and lingering suspicions about the motives of the Service, as leaders saw advantage in confidential contact.

One of the incentives was the offer of personal help to which the FRELIMO representative responded with a surprising request for

Tiger Balm. Asked why he wanted it, he said that it would enable them to run faster than the Portuguese. I wondered if he was pulling H/Lusaka's leg and later, back in HO, I asked a China expert for his opinion. He opened the drawer of his desk and took out a pot of Tiger Balm, saying that he used it himself. When tired and unable to concentrate on his work, he rubbed a little into his temples.

On to South Africa. I was met by H/Pretoria, the man whom I had chased up Whitehall in the training exercise. Confident and larger than life, he treated his role as a vehicle for self-expression. He had a bit of a swagger in contrast to the unassuming Head Office pen-wielder he took to meet General Hendrik Van den Bergh, head of the notorious Bureau of State Security. Just short of six foot six, Long Hendrik was a pillar of the Broederbond, the fellowship guarding the flame of Afrikaner destiny. Even when seated he tilted his head back and looked down his nose, his lips pursed in distaste. He welcomed me to South Africa and we talked generalities. Despite the political differences there were areas of shared concern and, in talking later to the two officers responsible for day-to-day contact, I saw that they enjoyed the inter-service camaraderie, palpably tinged with regret that we were not on their side.

I went on to the noise and bustle of Johannesburg, the hub of business in South Africa. The task of the station was to report on the evasion of the UN sanctions on trade with Rhodesia, ultimately a futile endeavour as no matter how much evidence was presented, trade passed unhindered through South Africa and Mozambique as neither country took action to stop it. Nevertheless, a continuing flow of reports was required to sustain the credibility of the UK as sponsor of the UN resolution, a task stoically borne by the service.

After two years I was suddenly dislodged from my comfortable niche and switched to desk officer for East and West Africa by the new C/Africa. Called to his office, I found him patrolling heaps of files laid out around his office which he picked up and slapped down. He had assembled every file in the office to do with Uganda, which he turned over to me with a wave of the hand. Uganda was in turmoil.

After a failed coup attempt, Amin was striking out in all directions. Two agents had fled and were in London.

It was a hard landing. In addition to force-feeding myself on Ugandan matters, I had to look after five other stations about which I knew next to nothing. I saw each of the two fugitive agents. My mind reeled as they recounted who said what to whom, why and when. I was telephoned at 4am by one of them, who had somehow found his way to New York and wanted support to return to Uganda with a group of rebels to overthrow Amin. The children, awakened, stood on the landing listening to me shouting down the phone forbidding some unknown person to go to Uganda.

After the dust had settled, I went out to Kampala to see how things were. I was captivated by Uganda, the very vision of the Africa of my imagination. Kampala was green, its hills laid out with gardens. Tall trees with monkeys and hornbills lined the streets and at five o'clock it rained for half an hour, the discharge of the daily evaporation from Lake Victoria. H/Kampala took me on a weekend trip to Lake Edward, renamed Lake Idi Amin, and I saw my other vision of Africa, the high dry savannah. Nearing the lake, we came upon a hippopotamus with a baby trotting alongside and two young lions trying to detach it from its mother.

On the surface, Uganda was little changed and, though shortages were developing, the worst ravages of Amin's reign had yet to come. The High Commissioner told a tale of the early days. On a Sunday afternoon, Amin's ADC telephoned to say that the President wished to see him and that he should bring his bathing costume with him. Amin was in his genial mood and they swam idly side-by-side. As they neared the end of the pool, the High Commissioner thought about the protocol aspects and, judging it inappropriate to arrive first, began to swim more slowly. Amin saw what the High Commissioner was up to and also swam more slowly, obliging the High Commissioner to reduce pace and so it went on, each countering the other until they hovered at the end of the pool.

I flew on to Kenya. While the Kampala station was back to square one, Nairobi was in full cry, so on top of their game that the Embassy had little to do. A visit to the game park, routine for visitors, was left for another occasion. Instead, I was taken racing by an officer, long serving in Kenya, who owned the back leg of a horse. We strolled into the owners' enclosure and sat in the stand overlooking the racecourse, immaculate in full colonial style. My companion told me tales of corruption and cheating despite which I allowed myself to be persuaded to place a bet on an outsider which, his sources informed him, was fixed to win. Needless to say, it did not.

Finally, on to Dar es Salaam and dusty workaday Africa. I reviewed the work of the station, called on liaison and talked with the High Commissioner. However, my abiding memory of the visit is of sitting next to Mrs H/Dar at breakfast, a fine figure of a woman barely contained in her skimpy bikini. Formally dressed for the day ahead, toast in hand, I could not think of anything to say.

Later, when the situation in Uganda had worsened to the point that there were fears for the safety of British subjects, contingency planning for a rescue mission was put in hand. I attended a meeting with the SAS with Peter de la Billière, then in command of A Squadron, in the chair. The Kampala station's contribution would be to shine a light to serve as a navigation beacon in the dropping zone. The SAS warned the Government that men could be lost to the crocodiles in Lake Victoria and the plan was dropped, so the station did not get to play its 'Allo 'Allo role.

I visited the three stations in West Africa. The glamour had gone out of these visits. They were work, travelling, living out of a suitcase, continually performing before strangers, including staff, many of whom were unknown to me. I began my round trip with Lagos, judging it likely to be the most demanding. I was met by a driver who, with a nod and a wink to officials, hustled me through Immigration and bundled me into the car. He caught the tail of a departing motorcade and we raced into Lagos with President Gowon. Lagos is not a sought-after posting. The climate is disagreeable and the city is ugly, sprawling, overcrowded, pulsing with life. I admired the staff and felt like a deserter when I left. In contrast to my speedy arrival, the car to the airport joined a convoy of cars escorted by the police for safety.

Accra had an altogether lighter and self-help atmosphere, perhaps spurious, which I found engaging. I met Ghanaians from the university, was introduced to local liaison at their headquarters in the historic slave fort and in the botanic garden I saw the tallest tree I have ever seen. In Dakar, it was hard-going for the station, confronted at every turn by French 'conseilleurs techniques'. The capital had style, with its tall aloof women and an ocean-side restaurant straight out of a James Bond film. It was so hot that we escaped from time to time to H/Dakar's car just to sit in the blast of its air-conditioner, at that time the very latest thing.

The 1970s were difficult years of social unrest, strikes, pay freeze and very cold winters. All three children were now at fee-paying schools, the cost of which was not fully covered by the boarding school allowances. We totted up on paper what we could afford and what not. I remortgaged the house but still we slid inexorably into debt. Twice I turned to my brother for rescue. Unmarried and living at home, he climbed and fished and drove big second-hand cars. When I telephoned him he knew why and brought his chequebook with him, signing away £200 a time, a hefty sum in those days.

Conventional holidays were out of the question but that was no impediment as we were a make-do and camping family. With our three animals on board, dog, guinea pig and gerbil, we set off in the overloaded Austin Cambridge for North Wales, our destination a campsite at Llewingwril, a village on the coast near Barmouth. The campsite was a large field in which sheep grazed. It had basic facilities only, namely toilets and a standpipe.

My wife and daughters had the large tent and my son and I shared the small mountain tent with the dog, which seemed a more companionable arrangement than sharing it with the two rodents. I had the dog on the lead round my wrist but such was its fidgeting

I detached it. I was woken up by barking and found the dog had gone, having gnawed its way out of the tent. Out in the rain in my underwear and bare feet, I chased the dog chasing the sheep, hissing its name, and tripping over the guys of tents in the dark. The following night the dog slept in the car and the rodents in the tent. There was more to come. On the eve of departure, we had a gala evening at Barmouth funfair. One of the girls won a goldfish in a little plastic bag which naturally had to come with us to Redhill and ended up on the sideboard.

On this and other holidays in Wales, the Lakes and Scotland, I tested my daughters to see if they had inherited the climbing gene. They enjoyed climbing the mountains and we had many fine days, though I had to bribe them to continue along the Crib Goch ridge when we tackled the Snowdon Horseshoe. I subjected both my daughters to rock-climbing. The younger one, though moving well, could not handle the exposure but the elder daughter showed encouraging signs and my hopes rose. We did two climbs on Tryfan in North Wales and two on crags in the Lakes but she could not get used to exposure. Only a partial transfer of the gene. My son was too young to be put to the test.

I got back into regular climbing about a year after my return from Tripoli. I joined the London Mountaineering Club and went along to an evening gathering at a London pub. I fell into conversation with Harry Woodbridge and we arranged to go on the next club meet in North Wales. We got on well, on and off the rocks, and formed a partnership that lasts to this day. I had done no rock-climbing in the six years of absence in Beirut and Libya and had to work my way up through the grades. There are many aspects to rock climbing and many explanations why it has such a hold on those who do it, but the effect on all is the same: it is an addiction and after the years of denial I was hooked again. In idle moments at work, I would practise traversing the office without touching the floor or a visitor would find me backing up in the doorway. My most taxing feat, not repeated, was to climb through a hatch between two rooms.

My second C/Africa moved on after barely a year and a third took his place, also new to me but I knew of him as Daphne's successor in the Congo. He divided his colleagues into pro-consuls, of whom he disapproved, and byzantines, of which he of course was one. He told me that his greatest satisfaction was to cause something to happen of which he was the unknown cause. He detected byzantine tendencies in me and increasingly drew me into his confidence. I started to stand in for him when he was away. The first time I made the weekly report to the Chief, it was at the killing after-lunch time of half past two and both the Chief, Maurice Oldfield, and the Director of Requirements dozed off. I allowed them ten minutes of blissful snuffling then roused them with a loud 'Finally Zambia'.

The months passed, then one day in late 1974 or early 1975, C/Africa said that he would like me to take over as the head of the Requirements, or reports, section. This was a surprise. I had never considered an R job, let alone as head of section. Of course, I accepted and I took charge of two desk officers and two cardists who in those pre-computer days noted items of interest too arcane for inclusion in the central card index.

I had by then been promoted to Grade 4 after some nineteen years in Grade 5, the incremental structure of which was said to be so long that nobody could live long enough to reach its end. I was very pleased with my enhanced status. The papers flowed across my desk but I was no longer at the coal-face. I attended the weekly Whitehall assessment meeting and made myself known to the Heads of African Departments in the Foreign Office. I sat at the Controller's desk in his absence.

As R/Africa I made further visits to stations in Africa (meeting in Lusaka a man whose name was Grey Zulu, a fit companion for Maroon Arab) and, from Lagos, flew on to Angola to look into the case for opening a station in Luanda, in view of concerns about Cuban involvement. I was handed a bag of onions to take to Luanda which, as predicted, was received with rapture. My hosts put on a dinner at which food and where to get it was almost the sole topic of conversation. Such food as could be found was obtained by barter with articles of clothing as the currency was worthless; the servant left her pay on the mantelpiece and took her breakfast home to feed the children. There was no sign of the Cubans and the city with its handsome buildings was a ghost town. In all, there was not a lot for an H/Luanda to work with.

In advance of a visit to Kinshasa I wrote to the Ambassador asking if there was anything I could bring out for him. He wrote back saying that if there was 'a tiny corner' in my suitcase he 'would love a small packet of All-Bran, not for the purpose you might suppose, but because it is my favourite cereal'. I formed a mental picture of the man whom I felt sure I was going to like.

The plane drifted down across the endless sprawl of Kinshasa's shanty town and back again to the airport. H/Kinshasa met me. I knew him; he was among the officers of former colonial services who joined the Service. We drove to his house which had been in station hands since the early days; it may have been Daphne's house, a small villa in what was a residential area of Belgian Leopoldville. It was now run down, the garden a dusty tangle of shrubs and the concrete water-tank abandoned with black streaks on its sides. The paved path continued into the house and we sat with our drinks each side of it, leaving the centre for the trail of droppings from the bats which swooped in and out of the house. In the kitchen, the stovepipe swarmed with translucent steam flies and, beside the stove, the kitchen implements lay in a greasy cardboard box. It was a dismal scene.

H/Kinshasa poured out all the problems he faced in making contacts in this disorganised country with its three or four languages, its obstructive and capricious officialdom, its suspicious population. His wife implored him to watch his words for his own sake. Her husband was past caring and, a little drunk, took me out for dinner. The restaurant was a bare open space with lights set on high poles like a sports pitch. The only diners, we sat in the muggy night with our beer, waiting and talking. A platter was brought heaped high with large unshelled brown prawns with a muddy, slightly off taste. I slept that night in a room with a barred window open to the air.

The Embassy occupied a suite in an office block in the centre of Kinshasa. The lavatories were out of order and staff had to use those of Barclay's Bank across the road. The Ambassador had a chemical toilet behind a screen in his room. At the end of work I went with him to his residence for lunch. As I expected, he was self-mocking and viewed the world calmly with an amused gaze. His wife, as if to order, was a small north-countrywoman exuding practicality.

After lunch we moved to the veranda which looked out over the vast Congo river, grey under the smouldering sky. Coffee was served and as we sat talking we heard the pinging of a hand-harp. 'C'est toi, Antoine?' 'Oui, Excellence, c'est moi,' replied the unseen Antoine in a deep voice and went pinging on his way. The setting and the scene could have come out of a Ronald Firbank novel. The Ambassador insisted on taking me back to H/Kinshasa's house and after driving up and down the featureless sixteen kilometre-long Avenue Kasavubu, unable to find the turn-off, he returned, defeated, to the Residence. 'Oh dear,' said his wife, 'come on, I'll drive you back.'

On return to London I recommended the closure of the station. H/Kinshasa was not getting anywhere and it was unlikely that a successor would fare any better. So, the rocket fired by Daphne fell to earth.

Northern Ireland

After six years of Africa I felt stirrings for a change and went to see Personnel. I found that my next move was not a live issue and the officer concerned promised to give it some thought and call me back. He did so a few days later: how about head of station Buenos Aires? Well, it was a handsome proposition but it was a non-starter as, somewhere on my file, there was the notice given me by the Head of Personnel after we returned from Tripoli that owing to my wife's fragile health I would not be posted overseas again. In any case it was not what I wanted to do. I had had my fill of casework and was thinking of something different, perhaps to do with politics, with Whitehall. As R/Africa, I was enjoying myself on the lower slopes of the uplands.

The following day, I was called back by the Personnel officer who by then had got the bit between his teeth. How about Northern Ireland? No shortage of politics there. I would be seconded to the Northern Ireland Office (NIO) and posted to the joint intelligence team in Stormont under a senior MI5 officer to explore ways of developing intelligence coverage. Well, the job was certainly out of the usual run and I went away to think about it.

To start with, it was not the sort of job that I visualised for myself and secondly, it was in Northern Ireland, the scene of seemingly endless bombings and violence to those watching television in England's quiet suburbs. Nevertheless, life went on and colleagues worked over there. Warming to the proposal, I felt that I would be letting myself down if I did not rise to the occasion. Moreover, there were positive personal considerations. It had elements of an overseas posting from which my wife was not barred as it was in the UK, it lifted me out of the commuting rut and the relentless round of gardening and DIY and, finally, there was good Irish rock to be climbed. My mind made up, I accepted.

The day came to cross the water. With the dog sedated on the back seat, my wife and I drove the lumbering Austin Cambridge in one long day to Belfast via Stranraer and Larne and, on arrival, were conducted to a house on the outskirts of Hollywood, a village swallowed up by Belfast. The small house had been furnished according to a list of entitlements for an officer of Counsellor rank and was so crammed with overstuffed armchairs and sofa, tables with lamps and beds close to the wall that there was little room to shuffle round. Much in need of a drink after unpacking ourselves and the dog, I went out to get a bottle. With some idea of the geography of the area I drove into the centre of Hollywood and found a pub. The moment I stepped through the door the noise and chatter stopped abruptly, all eyes turned to the interloper. Like a character in High Noon I walked to the bar and asked for a bottle of whisky, whereupon the regulars turned back to their drinks and the noise climbed to its previous level.

Might I have been an IRA gunman? Possibly, yes, but in a 'safe' Protestant area, highly unlikely. We had been advised to look for bombs under the car in the morning, which seemed good advice in London but a self-conscious and excessive precaution when no one around us was taking it. Away from the areas where the two communities rubbed shoulders, the everyday situation seemed normal and was superficially normal in those volatile areas but merely driving up the Falls Road increased the pulse rate. The mind was subconsciously on alert, and at times consciously. This was the normal.

I reported to my new boss, the senior MI5 officer, who as Director-General of Intelligence (DGI) represented intelligence in the upper counsels of the NIO and had broad oversight though not operational command of the staff of both services working in Northern Ireland. My first task was to make myself known to colleagues and to the Army and the police, the Royal Ulster Constabulary (RUC), with whom I was warned to tread cautiously as they were sensitive to meddling outsiders. After introductions at RUC headquarters, I was taken to lunch by a policeman twice my size and further intimidated by the huge steak placed before me which trailed over the ends of the oval plate. Pointing to the mountain of potatoes next placed on the table, my host, fixing me with an unwavering blue eye, said sternly 'Alec, these are Comber potatoes.' What did this mean? My mettle was being tested. Ah, yes, I said, and nodded.

I went on to develop an admiration for the RUC and got on easily with those with whom I worked, my principle contact being the Head of Special Branch (H/SB). With the pass I had been given to the headquarters, I could pop round to see him as required and enjoy a furtive wee dram. He invited me to his Christmas party, the only non-policeman. Fearing what lay ahead, I thought to make a modest start with a sherry, an improbable request in the circumstances, but H/SB saw through my ruse and presented me with a tumblerful of the stuff. Not unexpectedly, the evening ended with Irish coffee, after which Assistant Chief Constables and Chief Superintendents tumbled into the street past the midnight hour to find their cars' windscreens iced up. H/SB had the solution. He went back into the house and came back out with a washing-up bowl of hot water which he sloshed on the windscreens.

My main Army contact was the Colonel overseeing intelligence at Headquarters, and through him I saw how the Army was kept at work by pressure for action relentlessly pumped down the chain of command. They were critical of the more measured pace of their police counterparts and stories abounded of police officers playing golf when most needed. The Army was critical too of our failure to provide tactical intelligence to support their operations and put this down to lack of resolve, whereas it was due to the more strategic aim of our intelligence work. Talking to a group of officers on a social occasion I was berated for failing to exploit my freedom to cross the border. 'What do you expect me to do?' I replied, 'Prop up the bar of the Emerald Arms in Dundalk hoping to hear two Provos discussing the planned raid on the Cookstown post office'?

That was harsh and unfair but the Captain Nairac affair in May 1978 raised all these questions while providing no answers. The IRA abducted him from a South Armagh pub where, singing Republican songs, he was passing himself off as an IRA supporter, and took him across the border and executed him. Why did he do it? What was he hoping to achieve? To all appearances Nairac, whom I had met at an operational planning meeting, was a crisp and organised Army officer and certainly knew the risks as he was working in Army intelligence. The enquiry into responsibility for his death found that he had not sought approval for the operation as routinely required, which suggests that he knew it would be refused. There having been no risk assessment, the Army had little option but to draw a line under the incident while recognising the bravery of Nairac's action. He was posthumously awarded the George Cross.

Away from the office I took full advantage of the outdoor opportunities Northern Ireland offered. At the end of our road, a few minutes' walk, was Belfast Lough and along its shore I worked up a regular run of the six miles to Crawfordsburn and back, exhausting myself and the dog. I did some fell running in the Mourne mountains and took part in the annual Mourne Wall race. Soon after arrival, I joined the Belfast branch of the Irish Mountaineering Club, one of the two all-Ireland sporting associations, the other being for rugby. Catholics and Protestants, we all climbed together and had unforgettable but best forgotten evenings at the club hut in the Mournes, quaintly named The Bloat.

I went with a party to climb on the sea cliffs in west Donegal. We arrived late in the day at a hut, the club room of which contained no furniture other than the front seat of a car. For cooking, there were two blackened primus stoves, one standing on a greasy wine box turned on its side, the other beside it on the floor. My companions seemed to find things as expected and made a great play of hospitality, insisting that I sit in the car seat, effectively on the floor.

Hours passed. There were eight in the party and each of the four pairs took turns to cook elaborate fried meals of bacon, black pudding, eggs, sausages, and anything else that could be thrown in. As night closed in my hopes rose that we would be too late for the planned visit to a pub. But no: groaning with cramp I was helped to my feet and bundled into the car. My hopes rose again when I saw that the pub was in total darkness, only to fall again when my companions drove confidently into the parking area full of cars. After a tap on the window of the pub and brief scrutiny we joined the happy crowd within. Sh! Sh! We stood silent and still as the Garda rattled the door handle and checked the windows. Not long after the signal was given to resume merrymaking, there came a tapping on the window and two men wearing regulation green trousers were admitted.

The Club booked Peter Boardman of Himalayan fame to come to Belfast to talk about his ascent with Joe Tasker of the unclimbed West Wall of Changabang, the third highest Himalayan peak, which they climbed without support, alpine-style, the first such climb in the Himalayas. I became involved in the programme and on the day of his arrival I took him to lunch at Stormont, not grand but nevertheless an occasion for a visitor. His talk at Queen's University in the centre of Belfast started well over an hour late to no one's surprise except his. He was taken for a drink beforehand at a pub whose entrance was protected by a security enclosure. When they were admitted, the pub fell silent while they were scrutinised.

Boardman told me about this unnerving experience the following morning while we waited at the foot of a cliff on the Antrim coast without much enthusiasm for what lay ahead. In the mist coming off the sea, the rock was cold and damp. Among the assembled climbers was Calvin Torrance, the Joe Brown of Ireland, up from Dublin, to climb with Boardman. Saying goodbye in the late afternoon, as the party split up for departure, Boardman said that he had a flight to catch. Not a hope.

The children came out as usual for the holidays. We visited the Giants' Causeway and other must-see places in the North and had a camping holiday in Donegal. We sailed on Lough Neagh, my son tried rock climbing, my younger daughter passed her driving test which consisted of driving the examiner to his house, in which he spent ten minutes, then back to the test centre. However, despite all this enjoyable activity we did not settle as a family, putting down roots as we did on overseas postings. There was little sense of home. We only came together for holidays and the house was holiday accommodation, in which for the most part I dwelt alone with the dog. My wife preferred to remain in London, where we were in the process of setting up a new home.

The posting to Ireland had brought into focus the question of what to do about the house in Redhill. We had not wanted to rent it out after what had happened last time but equally it was undesirable to leave it unattended for an extended period. Furthermore, the house was larger than we now needed as the girls had gone on their way. These musings led us to the decision to sell the house and buy something smaller that was simpler to run. The question of where to seek this desirable property was not an issue: it had to be in London and as close to the office as possible. After the pleasant morning drive to Stormont, I was not going back to commuting. Without too much of a search, we settled on a small terrace house with garage and off-street parking on the fringes of Camberwell, a short drive to the office. After we moved in I found three colleagues lived in the same road, a veritable nest of spies

In 1977, in a reshuffle of roles, I became A/DGI, Assistant to DGI, in a new appointment. He transferred to me such day-to-day oversight of intelligence activities as he exercised, which left him free to enjoy his role in the top team advising the minister. Internment had been ended, and in January 1977 the decision was taken to restore the primacy of the police. Way Ahead studies were commissioned, and the one for intelligence was given to me to write. The RUC appointed a Superintendent to liaise with me and at the first meeting he made his position crystal clear. He announced, 'Alec, there are to be no committees. Committees are a waste of time.'

Though the Way Ahead was clear enough, I took to the road to visit regional RUC headquarters and Army bases, collecting the views of Chief Superintendents and Brigadiers. There were already in existence local arrangements for the exchange of intelligence and all that was needed was to formalise them and set up regional 'groups' (committees) under RUC chairmanship to oversee them and review arrangements periodically. The only bone of contention was that between SB and CID over the ownership of information of security interest acquired by CID. In the report, I attempted to distinguish between criminal and security intelligence without any expectation that it would end the contention, which I expect is widespread in the police. My anodyne report with its predictable recommendations was sucked into the paper maw without comment.

I was flattered to be included in the guest list of a small dinner party attended by the Chief Justice, the Permanent Secretary of the NIO, the Chief Constable, DGI and other luminaries. I was placed between two ladies, on my right the wife of the Chief Constable, the one on my left I never discovered, as I became hopelessly entangled with Mrs Newman, spouse of Kenneth, the future Commissioner of the Metropolitan Police. To converse with her, who was sitting on my deaf side, I had to shuffle half right and screw my head round to present my working left ear. Stuck for conversation, I talked about climbing, which led from Ireland to London and to the climbing wall at the Sobell Centre. Mrs Newman asked its whereabouts and my reply that it was five minutes' walk from Finsbury Park tube station sparked her interest. 'Why, that's Kenny's old manor,' she exclaimed and proceeded to question me about its precise location. I knew how to get there but not the address. She threw one street name after another at me to no avail. I looked round and saw grave men talking and nodding wisely while I was trapped in an A to Z quiz.

I changed the subject. I asked if she had family. Yes. In Belfast? Yes. At school? No. Taught at home? Yes. Some parent home education scheme? No. Ever been to school? No. What never? Well, only for one day. One day!? For obedience training. The dog.

In London, the posting wheel turned and my time in Ireland came to an end. The A/DGI appointment had taken root and I was succeeded by an MI5 officer. I sat late into the night with him, pouring out all my knowledge and experience and saw it trickle away. It was ever thus: he would do the job as he found it. I saw myself off at the airport the following day.

I returned to our new house in London in which I was to live alone. Some months earlier, my wife had suffered a serious breakdown and was in hospital. It had happened when she was alone in London and was found by her step-mother who went to the house at my insistence after a worrying telephone call. Yet again she was driven down by the depression that haunted her, despite all the treatment she had received and the medication which was as much a trap as a help. Yet again, she spent long periods of rehabilitation in one hospital or another but, this time, did not return to herself.

A change of direction

Once again, I sat across the desk from the Personnel Officer: what next? Some thought had been given to this as he offered me a choice: either head of the UK station working on African targets or first holder of a newly created appointment, R/Coordination. The latter job seemed to be that of assistant to the Director of Requirements to do those parts of his job he found uncongenial, while the former was Africa again. With a sigh, I chose the Africa job. It lacked novelty but it was a real job, whereas the other was untried and indeed proved short-lived.

Not long in my new job and quite unexpectedly, I went out to Rhodesia as a member of a small diplomatic mission to observe the election to approve the power-sharing deal negotiated between Bishop Muzorewa and the Smith government. The inclusion of an SIS member was at the insistence of David Owen, the Foreign Minister, who was going through a phase of frustration with the Foreign Office, describing its officials as behaving like parish councillors. He even went so far as to telephone the desk officer for Southern Africa, which was shocking and unheard of and, in turn, obliged the Chief to report to the Permanent Secretary what his minister was up to behind their backs.

The election was a charade as the leaders of the two organisations fighting the bush war, ZANU and ZAPU, denounced the power-sharing deal and instructed their followers to boycott the election. The reduced electorate, largely white, voted 82% in favour and the new state of Zimbabwe Rhodesia was duly proclaimed but immediately met with international rejection. All this was played out in the media and the only thing the mission could observe was that the election had been conducted decorously in the capital.

It was of course interesting to visit the Forbidden Territory. Salisbury had an old-fashioned air redolent of the colonial era. I did not visit the African townships but I drove round the white suburbs with their comfortable houses, big gardens, and barking dogs partly out of curiosity, partly to confirm that I was not under surveillance and partly with a view to possible future operations. An Intelligence Officer Never Sleeps. With colleagues I visited the famous Meikles Hotel, steeped in history, where we sat in the 1920s lounge murmuring over tea to the tinkle of a piano.

In a further effort to find a solution, the Government summoned all parties to the conflict to a conference in London. In September 1979, the Lancaster House Conference began its lengthy proceedings which ended in the creation of the Republic of Zimbabwe with Robert Mugabe as Prime Minister. The Service, with its contacts among the African parties, played a role behind the scenes.

It fell to me to handle one of these contacts. I was introduced to him over lunch at Wheeler's in St James's by the colleague who had formed the relationship with him during his service in Africa. The two were pleased to see each other and during the protracted catch-up of news the waiter was repeatedly sent away. Finally the frosty maître d'hôtel came to demand our order. Our African friend looked up and, with a straight face, asked innocently, 'Do you have any mealie?' I saw him repeatedly during the three months of the conference and we became at ease with each other. He did not see himself as an agent, more a co-conspirator. I saw him of course under alias.

The Case of the Wandsworth Soothsayer began with the prison drawing the attention of Special Branch to a letter addressed to a white prisoner from Colonel Acheampong, the President of Ghana. The Branch passed the letter to us and an officer went to see the prisoner. It transpired that, nearing the end of his sentence, he had set himself up as a soothsayer and had acquired two clients, the Zaire Ambassador in London and Colonel Acheampong. The letter in question sought to know the prisoner's vibrations about the man selected for appointment as Minister of Commerce. The prisoner explained that he simply wrote back at whim.

The ability to manipulate the President of Ghana by controlling the prisoner's vibes naturally appealed to us and, finding nothing to discredit the proposed Minister of Commerce, we instructed the prisoner to feel positive vibes. This fairy-tale case did not last long. After he came out of prison, the prisoner tried to screw money out of us and we left Col Acheampong and the Zaire Ambassador to his caprice.

In 1980 I was summoned by the Head of Personnel who, without preamble and out of the blue, offered me the appointment of Head of Training Department (HTD). I returned to my office walking on air. What a surprise, both the appointment and the promotion. Training had never entered my thoughts and the promotion marked a significant advance in my career and cleared my mind of second thoughts about the choice of job I had made on return from Ireland. Taking charge of the Training Department was the challenge ahead and I felt the familiar tingle of apprehension.

The staff of Training Department was divided between London and Fort Monckton, the famous 'spy school' on the south coast, its official MOD cover long blown. It had not achieved notoriety in my day though the local population knew its role and conspired to keep its cover, rather proud to have it in their locality. It was rather splendid to live and work within the walls of an 18th century fort. The wide parade ground was fringed with the buildings required to house and support the flow of trainees, ours, from other services and from overseas. For some colleagues the Fort was the heart of the service. For my part, whilst acknowledging its talismanic status, I found it rather cold and uncomfortable and, despite my powers as HTD, I was unable to change the straitjacket bed-making of the ex-RN orderlies.

The role of HTD was administrative and representational, the latter function exercised principally at the Fort. I presided when the occasion demanded: the presence of senior Whitehall or Armed Forces figures, senior overseas liaison visitors, the new entrants end-of-course dinner and so on. My lecturing role was limited to delivering a set-piece talk entitled 'The Role and Functions of SIS' to officers at Staff College whose eyes glazed over after the opening remarks. Visiting senior liaison figures were a strain. For support in the conversation marathon, I worked up a short presentation on the qualities SIS looked for in an intelligence officer. The first time I drew on it was after lunch with the Deputy Head of the Indian Security Service who promptly fell asleep.

The Head of the Egyptian Service, however, hung on to my words, his gaze unfocussed as if beholding a vision. 'Finally' I concluded, 'Integrity', whereupon he gave a deep sigh. So impressed was he that shortly afterwards an invitation came for me to visit Cairo to give the same talk to his officers. It was not a success. The audience seemed to be a group of mid-ranking officers attending a course. They arrived altogether in a hurry after the appointed time in no mood to listen as it was well past lunchtime.

The Egyptian escorting officer was a cosmopolitan Cairene with perfect English. I was taken by him and a colleague to dinner and show at a Cairo nightspot. The table was right up against the little stage affording a closer than wanted view of the wobbling belly-dancers. My companions spoke freely and frankly about Arab affairs and their own government. I wondered if H/Cairo heard such talk. I got on so well with my bear-leader that at the end of the visit I gave him my telephone number in London. I was not travelling under an alias.

The unexpected happened, he telephoned some months later.

I invited him to dinner and rustled up a couple of colleagues to form a four for bridge as during my visit to Cairo he told me that he regularly played at a Cairo club, occasionally partnering Omar Sharif. Camberwell and partnering me was a bit of a come-down but the game's the thing. In the course of the evening I mentioned that my daughter, studying History of Art at Edinburgh University, was planning to visit Cairo to compare the form of Fatimid and Abbasid windows for her thesis, an arcane subject to be sure. My Egyptian friend immediately suggested and insisted that she stay with his family; and so she did.

Within months of the Zimbabwean Government taking office, the first batch of trainees from the new security service arrived for training. The Minister for Security, Emerson Mnangagwa, came to see them at the Fort. He was accompanied by a white officer and, over dinner, the two ribbed each other and laughed about an occasion when Mnangagwa narrowly escaped capture, this coming from a man who had spent years in prison and was only spared execution because of his youth. Remarkable.

The following morning I showed him to the students' classroom. On entering all stood and, fists raised, chanted the ZANU slogan. I made to leave with the instructor but Mnangagwa stopped us. He addressed the students in Shona, then quizzed them in English for our benefit on the threats to Zimbabwe from its neighbours, causing surprise when he did not exclude any neighbour as a potential threat. I saw Mnangagwa again a couple of years later in Zimbabwe. We met for tea at Meikles Hotel, piano tinkling away, to discuss a project of H/Harare's requiring local support. Mnangagwa was as expansive as earlier, in his thirties, a young, exciting leader. That was before it all went wrong. Now President of Zimbabwe he has the opportunity to redeem himself.

I found HTD a demanding appointment, not the administrative side but the representational role and, while I became more practised at it, it was no hardship to give it up when my time came to an end in 1982 with my appointment as Controller Africa. It was hardly a surprise. If ever a man was prepared for the position, that man was I, the only missing element in my formation being service in Africa itself. If no surprise, it was nonetheless very satisfying to have climbed to a pinnacle that was beyond ambition at the outset of my career.

An Indian interlude

During my spell as HTD an invitation came from my Australian counterpart to visit the training department in Melbourne. It seemed that an exchange of such liaison visits occurred from time to time and, whilst agreeing with the Director of Administration, under whom I came, that they were totally unnecessary, it was an opportunity to break free from routine for a while and to see a world I did not know. To win him over, I expanded the visit to include fly-by stops in India, Kuala Lumpur, Singapore, and Hong Kong, from all of whom we received trainees. Still unpersuaded, my superior nevertheless gave way, marvelling at my willingness to sacrifice myself on the altar of entertainment by liaison services.

The visit to India was more than a fly-by occasion. One of the training staff at the Fort had long been involved in support for the Indian stay-behind organisation formed to operate in the event of incursion of the northern border. The Service had helped to create this organisation, essentially a peasant army of unimaginable numbers, and my colleague was due to make one of his regular visits. The plan was that I would join him in Delhi and go with him to the training base near the north-west frontier.

I spent two or three days in Delhi looked after by Indian liaison colleagues. I was taken to see the Red Fort and the Taj Mahal which I cannot say was disappointing, only that it was less romantic than the pearly Taj Mahal of imagination, and less pristine than hoped for as the endless stream of visitors had left a patina of grease on the marble. Still, the monkeys were there and the throng, ebullient and noisy. The drive back through Agra was total immersion in India. With the driver hooting continually we drove slowly through the heedless crowd, negotiating oncoming vehicles and a bullock-drawn cart along streets lined with hawkers of sweets displaying loops of orange and red jelabi. In the evening I was taken out to dinner. On leaving the restaurant we were accosted by an armless beggar. He wore a short cape held up by the stumps of his arms on which to catch donations. My companion tossed him a worthless coin which he flicked up into his mouth and rattled into position with those already there.

H/Delhi, known behind his back as Captain Birdseye, gave a dinner party attended by Indian colleagues. After the meal, to fill the entertainment void, he showed a film of an improving nature sent out by London and, at the end of it, he offered to follow on with a film about elections in Zimbabwe, possibly those I had attended. To the relief of all, the wife of one of the Indian officers had the courage to stand up and declare, 'All good things must come to an end.'

My colleague from the Fort ducked out of all this entertainment and only reappeared for the onward journey to the training camp. We were picked up by the headquarters officer detailed to escort me, a modest and undemanding Sikh, his cheeks pushed up under his eyes by the tight net holding his beard. We travelled by helicopter and jeep and on what remained of the first day I was shown round and shook hands.

On the afternoon of the second day, I was to see a demonstration of a river crossing, the swimmers supported by improvised buoyancy aids in the torrential current. The morning programme slipped and lunch trailed on so that it was late afternoon when we set off on the long drive down to the river. In the gathering dusk, we were shown to a row of seats in a clearing out of sight from the river which we could hear. After a while the floodlight under which we were sitting was turned off, and we sat in total darkness and silent anticipation. The light was switched back on and before us stood two men, water streaming off them, standing to attention and saluting with one hand and clutching an inflated animal bladder in the other. I went over to them and shook their hands. I examined the bladders, cooing my admiration of their feat. For all we had seen, the men could just as well have been doused by a bucket of water.

On the morning of the last day I attended the enactment of the interception of a stay-behind agent. First, a peasant trudged into view carrying a bundle of firewood, then a soldier in uniform burst on the scene, shouting and knocking the peasant down. The soldier searched the peasant, examined the firewood, kicked the peasant, and walked off. My turn came next. I was invited to examine the firewood in which a message had been concealed. I submitted twig after twig to feigned close scrutiny after which I gave up, which I was bound to do even if I had spotted anything. A member of the staff then made play of looking through the firewood then, selecting a piece, carefully drew out a tiny piece of paper from under the bark. It was barely large enough for two letters but, with Indians capable of inscribing the Qur'an on a grain of rice, who knows what was possible.

Weary of attention, I took leave of the Commandant and shook hands with the entire staff of the establishment down to the last kitchen hand before getting into the jeep with my quiet and constrained Sikh who lived, so he had told me, entirely on a diet of chapatis and dal. However, the Commandant and his deputy also climbed into the jeep and at the helicopter pad I again shook hands with them and the driver and boarded the helicopter with my Sikh escort. My spirits sank when the Commandant followed me on board. In Delhi I said goodbye to him for the third time and, at the airport, bade farewell to my faithful Sikh companion. According to the goodbye rate of attrition I expected to see him also on board the plane but no, I was alone in the hands of Air India, mindful of the advice to make an early visit to the toilet.

The remainder of the trip was characterised by heroic eating as predicted. In Kuala Lumpur, the delicious prawns I had for dinner so disagreed with me that on the way to give an address at the training school I stopped the car to be sick in the gutter. In Singapore, I was treated to a substantial lunch at the famous Raffles Hotel and, in Hong Kong, managed to drop some abalone in my lap, despite using a fork, making a horrible mess on my trousers. Some good came of my stay, though, as I was measured for a suit by S K Charlie, Custom Tailor, sent to London without a fitting. I still wear it.

However, it was in Australia that I was put to the severest test. In the name of hospitality (and to teach this Pommie a thing or two) my hosts amused themselves by overloading my plate. The programme included a night's camping in the bush. After a gargantuan first course and copious wine I was presented with half a large melon filled to the brim with port. Barely able to focus my eyes, the spectacle of the night sky made it all worthwhile.

Controller Africa

It was very nice, being a Controller. It had a certain cachet; it was the most dashing of HO appointments. We were the Squadron-Leaders: above us Group-Captains sat in stuffy desk jobs but we had the skies. We gathered once a month for lunch in the Chief's dining room and very pleased with ourselves we were, lolling about like lords of creation.

The out-going C/Africa insisted on the need for a farewell tour and that I should go with him to ensure continuity despite my being a familiar figure on the Africa circuit. So it came to pass. I was well used to the mercurial ways of my companion from my time in the UK station with him as Controller and the two-man act was as gruelling as I expected.

We were spared one leg of the trip by the chance presence in London of the President of Malawi, Dr Banda. A meeting was arranged. We reported to the hotel at which he was staying and were met by the Malawian Cabinet Secretary who was to attend the meeting. After some time, a uniformed ADC entered and stood to attention in the doorway. We rose, an ill-assorted trio, to find ourselves facing a mirror and casting furtive glances to avoid eye contact with each other. Dr Banda walked in slowly and we shook hands. The ensuing conversation wended its way to the affinity of the Ndei dialect with Zulu with examples.

The out-going C/Africa suggested that I join the Travellers' Club. Many of our FCO colleagues were members and it was a suitable place to entertain and have a quiet chat about this and that in safe surroundings. Very persuasive; other members of the Service also found membership useful. I let myself be persuaded and after the palaver of finding sponsors and seconders I became a member, whereupon I was berated by my daughters who disapproved, accusing me of betraying my class origins. Feeling an imposter, I set about exploiting the operational tool I had acquired. I marched in expecting to be directed to the tradesman's entrance and waited for my guest in the cavernous hall. After the obligatory unwanted drink at the bar, we found our place at a separate table in the dining room, in the centre of which there stretched a long refectory table at which diners sat, as if back at school or college.

It was all in vain, for as we started our quiet chat I could not make out what my guest was saying. I could only hear the voice of Sir Ralph Richardson, lunching at a nearby table, rising above the busy murmur. Fiddling with my hearing aid did not help and the nods and grunts with which I habitually covered my hearing loss did not help either as the purpose of the lunch was to hear what my guest had to say. Defeated by deafness, I resigned from the club, forfeiting the entry fee but regaining the regard of my daughters. Instead I gave lunch in my office: smoked salmon, cambazola and grapes, washed down by a premier cru Chablis. Deputy and Assistant Undersecretaries, Ambassadors and High Commissioners all came and we could talk away at the top of our voices.

I continued to get away for long weekends with Harry Woodbridge. The rock-climbing was going well, we were 'pushing the grades' as climbers say. We were climbing E1 (Extreme Grade 1) regularly and broke through into E2 with a famous Joe Brown climb, the 'Mighty Vector', as it was hailed in the first guide-book of the area. I did not allow my lofty status to constrain my in-office gymnastics. I added to my repertoire a handstand balanced on the back and seat of a chair and could be found feet in the air.

I made a plan to climb Mt Kenya with my daughter, taking advantage of her presence in East Africa. She had finished at university and was on a no-frills safari ending in Nairobi and I timed a visit to Africa to coincide. We went on a three-day guided ascent of Point Lenana at 16,355 ft, one of the four subsidiary peaks surrounding the rocky summit. Mt Kenya is an extinct volcano whose lava outflow extends many miles in all directions so that, seen from afar, the outline of the mountain looks like a boil swelling to a pimple. On the first day, we mounted steadily through thinning vegetation to the foot of the steep final section. Booted and dressed for the mountain, we were put to shame by our guides wearing plastic flip-flops. They put up a tent to which I withdrew feeling ill, further put to shame by my daughter, fresh from Kilimanjaro, unaffected by the altitude. The following day we scrambled up to Point Lenana. All I could think about was getting off the mountain as quickly as possible so we hurried on down, reducing our three-day tour to two.

Back at the office and looking at the list of those attending the Royal College of Defence Studies course I saw that there was a Nigerian colonel among them. I telephoned him, told him who I was and said that I would like to meet him. At his suggestion, we met for tea after Friday prayers at the hotel across the road from the mosque in St John's Wood. I had, of course, an intelligence objective but from the outset I decided, drawing on my experience of Africans (and of Arabs), to see how things might develop on the basis of shared interest in the contact and the growth of personal relations. I did not therefore ask any leading questions and kept patiently to the progress of his course, life in London, his family, children's education and so forth. We met about once a month.

A dramatic event occurred towards the end of June 1984. A Customs Officer at Stanstead Airport acting on information located a large crate awaiting shipment as diplomatic freight to Lagos. When opened, the crate was found to contain a drugged and insensible man later identified as Umaru Dikko, a prominent Nigerian opposition figure. 'The Man in the Box' story was all over the newspapers.

I knew from our conversations that my Nigerian contact was close to the military leadership of the country and was therefore a channel for off-the-record communication. I passed this on to the FCO and my moment of glory had arrived. I attended a meeting with Geoffrey Howe, Foreign Secretary, in the chair, Leon Brittan, Home Secretary, Malcolm Rifkind, Minister of State at the Foreign Office, Norman Tebbit, Trade and Industry Secretary, the Private Secretary from No 10 and three Heads of Department from the FCO.

The meeting started with a protracted investigation of how diplomatic cargo could be recognised, finally settled by Norman Tebbit drawing on his days as a pilot, then turned to whether the state had the authority to open such cargo. As these matters were batted to and fro, Rifkind became increasingly agitated and finally broke in to say that surely there was a humanitarian obligation to open the box. He was put down at once by Howe, who said that that was another matter.

Eventually the question of what should be done was raised. The meeting seemed to have no idea other than reciprocal withdrawal of Heads of Mission and I piped up that I could attempt to get a reaction to this proposed course of action. The offer was taken up and Howe riffled through his diary. He would like a reply by Tuesday as he would be speaking in the House that day. It was Friday and, as I searched for words, Tebbit drawled, 'You'll be lucky to get any reply at all.' And on that note the meeting ended.

I got in touch with my Nigerian contact. An affirmative answer came back promptly and Howe made his statement. My contact told me that a delegation of notables would come to London on a goodwill mission and, days later, three elderly grey-beards in voluminous robes and headdresses arrived. They were grave and silent. Nobody quite knew who they were or what to do with them. I set up a meeting on our premises with Rifkind whom the visitors inspected with curiosity, if not suspicion.

When it was all over the Chief said to me that it was the best thing I had ever done. After twenty nine years of toil this rather annoyed me but maybe he was right. Had I at last learned the power of restraint, tea and small talk? Months later, I received a bulky package containing a Morocco leather pouffe in Nigeria's national colours, green and yellow, on which were embroidered the words 'Thankyou Mr McOnald'.

Towards the end of my time as C/Africa I made two farewell visits to Africa, the first to East and West Africa. In Lagos I made a farewell call on the head of the Nigerian Security Service whom, for one reason or another, I had not previously met. The meeting took place not in his office but at his house in Lagos, a large dusty villa watched over by his retinue and uniformed guards. I was impressed. He was a senior figure by virtue of his office but it seemed that he was rather grander and had status in Hausa society. He received me affably and we were talking over a glass of Coca-Cola when a man on his hands and knees appeared at the open door of the room and held up an envelope. My host gestured him to put it on a side table, whereupon the man crawled on his hands and knees to obey then crawled out backwards.

The second of my farewell visits was to South Africa, taking in Angola and Botswana on the way. In Angola we had opened a station and I wanted to see how H/Luanda, a young officer under official cover, was getting on. I also looked forward to staying with old friends from Tripoli days, the Head of Chancery and his wife, installed as Mr and Mrs Ambassador. We sat drinking tea in the Embassy garden in the shade of the Livingstone Tree, under which the explorer had sat recovering from malaria.

The visit to Botswana was exploratory. After the ghost town of Luanda, the capital Gaborone was full of life just as in the books Alexander McCall Smith had yet to write. I had an enjoyable exchange with the Chief of Police. To flatter him, I told him he looked too young for so important a post and added that he looked younger when he told me he was forty-two. He then asked my age and I told him, fifty-three. 'I thought you were older,' he said, somehow getting his compliment wrong.

On to Pretoria to meet the new head of BOSS, Dr Niels Barnard. Instead of the expected office meeting I found that I was invited to dinner at his home in Bronkhorstspruit, fifty kilometers from Pretoria. In the presence of several members of his staff, Barnard began, 'I have no reason to love the British,' and continued that his father had been among those held in a British concentration camp. Developing a different theme, he then spoke passionately about Africa. 'I am an African,' he said, 'the everyday concerns of Africans are my concerns'. I did not doubt the sincerity of his plea for understanding of Afrikaners and their predicament but it could not change the politics and, as the atmosphere became less charged, we drifted back to the usual exchange of views and the conviviality of the traditional barbecue.

At the end of my visit the South Africans saw me off in style. They insisted on taking me to the airport and in the VIP lounge presented me with a bottle of fifty-three year-old brandy with a suspiciously new label. I was driven to the plane minutes before take-off and escorted to my seat. The passengers fell silent, assuming I was being deported.

I was due to retire in a year's time and my thoughts turned to what I would do in the thereafter. It was common practice for my colleagues to take up jobs as advisors or security experts. My predecessor as Head of Training telephoned one day to say that he was approaching retirement from Gallagher's, the tobacco company, where he was in charge of security. They were good to work for, the job was varied and interesting and there was a pension. Was I interested? I met him and a director of Gallagher's for lunch at a London club and learned a few days later that the job was mine.

Perhaps having got wind of this, Personnel invited me to stay on for a further three years. I had a year earlier been invited to become the terrorism boffin of the Service for as long as I chose. I had turned it down without a second thought. Wrong man: I could not become one of the grey academics we had in the office, forever lecturing, attending conferences and meetings, not to mention the mental strain of keeping abreast of the subject. The job proposed by Personnel was C/UK in charge of operations in the UK. I was flattered. It was a handsome and suitable job but I knew what it entailed and I simply did not want to do it. Even the hint of possible further promotion did not tempt me. I had had enough. I had glimpsed the Elysian fields beyond.

A few days later, the Head of Personnel came to my office and asked if I would like my name to be put forward for the post of Director-General of the Internal Security Department of Oman. I was astounded. I knew that the Service had provided officers for this appointment in this fabled land where, legend had it, you needed the Sultan's permission to own a radio and had to carry a lantern at night. It had never entered my mind to aspire to this appointment and, though I knew that I could not turn down this amazing proposition, I needed to let it sink in. I am not excitable by nature and was able to tell the Head of Personnel calmly that I would think about it and give him an answer the next day.

As soon as the coast was clear, I popped along to the office library and pulled out an atlas. Were there any mountains? Yes, mountain ranges 10,000 ft high and deserts and sea. That clinched it. I put out of my mind whether I could handle the responsibility and the Arab workforce, taking the down-to-earth rock-climber's view that it was no use worrying about third pitch if you could not get off the ground.

My life changed. I was introduced to the visiting Head of the Palace Office, the man to whom I would routinely report. The Chief gave him lunch, Controller Middle East on his left, the visitor on his right with me next to him. The Chief's steward poured the wine and totally missed the visitor's glass. The spilt wine fountained off the polished surface of the table, sparkling in the sunlight like a television advert. The visitor affected not to notice and carried on talking to the Chief as the steward came and went with a cloth to mop up.

The next step was to go out to Oman for the National Day celebrations in November to be seen and approved. I was the guest of the Palace Office and endured hours of entertainment by its staff. With them I watched the parade and the ceremonies and, for light relief, the Cup Final. To keep the crowd happy, the teams came on the pitch three times to warm up and it is a wonder they had anything left by the time the Sultan arrived and the game began with cries of goal, shoot (pron. esh-oot) and corner. The following day, at the Tea Party, which forms part of the celebrations, I was introduced to the Sultan and given the nod.

I handed over my job at year's end and prepared myself for Oman, reading files and studying Arabic. I would be the third Director-General from the Service and also the last, since my task was to complete the Omanisation of the Service. In the 1985 New Year's Honours I was awarded the CMG. In due course I went to the Palace with my three children to receive the medal from the Queen. It would not lie flat on its ribbon and she poked at it in a grandmotherly way.

Oman

I flew out to Oman on 1st April 1985. As we sat waiting for take-off, I was asked if I would be prepared to give up my seat and move to Club to make way for a passenger who customarily travelled with two seats. I refused and refused again when a further attempt to unseat me was made. A while later I stood up to allow a large elderly man access to the window seat. Passengers came from across the cabin to greet him but he did not introduce himself to me. Little did I know that I was sitting next to the Sultan's uncle, the Deputy-Prime Minister for Defence and Security. When in due course I called on him in my official capacity he exclaimed 'Ha! It's you. I know you.'

On landing, the welcoming party were waiting for me on descent from the plane and my life changed. I became a VIP. I was not allowed to carry anything. I was served coffee and dates in the VIP lounge while my passport was rushed through Immigration. I felt embarrassed not only by all this attention but also perversely by my inability to be more demanding to satisfy the eagerness to serve of the welcoming party. After the drive to Internal Security Department (ISD) headquarters and further courtesies, I was at last left alone in a guesthouse on the camp.

The guesthouse was one of two in an enclave on the edge of the bluff overlooking the small township of Madina Qaboos. It was surrounded by gardens with flowering trees and, round the pool, by jasmine and queen of the night, fragrant on the night air. The following morning, awake early, I sat on the veranda in my pyjamas listening to the call to prayer taken up by one mosque after another, transported to another world. I had with me no possessions other than a few clothes and books and felt free, released, and open to what lay ahead.

I felt confident I could handle the work. The service had been set up and run by British officers, the last two of which were SIS colleagues who had no more and probably less experience than I had. I would be getting into a warm bed. I would of course be subjected to scrutiny by some 1,800 strangers but the initial awkwardness would pass. The staff, expatriate and Omani, would have to take me as they found me, after all I was the boss. The question was: could I handle the role?

I knew, but not well, the colleague I was to succeed. He greeted me on arrival but we spent no time together, so busy was he clearing his desk and making his farewells that it was not until the eve of his departure that we finally sat down together. His valedictory report was that the Head Office was ticking over with expatriate support, the outlying stations were less effective, while the service as a whole was weighed down by unproductive staff recruited in the early days. He ended with a warning that never left my mind. He said, 'You are surrounded by heffalump traps and you won't know if you fall into one.'

The following day, I shook hands with the senior officers when they assembled for the morning meeting. I made a short speech in which I spoke of the privilege of the appointment, my orders to Omanise the service, and my promise to serve in the interests of all as an honorary Omani. As such I did indeed regard myself as I had taken the Sultan's shilling. I was not on secondment and I had no intention of allowing myself to be drawn into an agent type relationship (heffalump trap territory). I was the head of a liaison service and, as such, I would manage my dealings with SIS and CIA. I well understood the requirements of both services and anything they needed to know I would tell them.

The bed was even warmer than I expected. The service was modelled on SIS. The offices around the country were called stations with station commanders reporting to controllers. HO notices were graded List A and List B, a system of my own invention when I was staff-officer to the Vice-Chief twenty-five years earlier. I found two former colleagues among the expatriate staff and, astonishingly, my secretary was none other than the one I had in Northern Ireland. There appeared to be no dress code for male expatriates. They seemed dressed for the beach in short-sleeved shirts, on one wearer open to the midriff on which a chunky gold chain dangled. My first act as DG was to issue an order requiring expatriate officers to wear a long-sleeved shirt and tie to work.

The question of where I was to live had to be decided. My predecessor had lived in a villa in a fashionable area with his wife and daughter, a maid, a cook, and a houseboy. The villa, too big for my needs, was dwarfed by the next house I was shown, a small palace suitable for an Omani grandee. It had a kitchen to cook for a hundred and a huge majlis, the Arab sitting room with cushions along the walls. To the bewilderment of the Omani staff, I rejected status and decided to stay put and live on the camp in the other larger guesthouse.

Consternation! I thought it perfect. To me, it was a villa on the Côte d'Azure. It was quite big enough; it was secluded and inaccessible to casual visitors (heffalump trap). The Administration Department went into overdrive. The bungalow had to be refurbished and the ceilings raised which involved taking the roof off. My protests were brushed aside. My Omani deputy explained to me that I was not behaving in a manner befitting my status and, though he did not say it, that I should put up and shut up and graciously comply.

The Headquarters had been built in the early 1970s on undeveloped land and, thanks to the vision of the founding fathers, we had a large camp in a fine position with a good HO building and a whole range of outlying buildings: the Officers' Club and pool, messes for junior staff, workshops, gym, mosque, staff housing, clinic and the guest houses. I made my way round inspecting the various sections. I was surprised to find that Training Section consisted of one ex-Intelligence Corps sergeant. I called up the files to find out why this was so and learned that my predecessor had commissioned a review of training requirements and had agreed with the report's conclusion that the training of the Service was 'complete'. An incomprehensible decision. The only training provided by the lone sergeant was an induction course for new staff based on the training manual written by a visiting SIS officer in the early days. The first section of the first module gives an idea of how long ago that was: it was headed 'Why do we use paper'.

I visited the stations which, unlike those in SIS, were not hidden away but existed in full sight in camps with uniformed guards and the full range of supporting staff. Whatever their effectiveness, I saw that with the police, the military and the Wali, the civil Governor, they were part of the manifestation of the state. On public occasions the head of station sat in the front row with the Wali and other dignitaries. The stations thus embedded in the community were well able to monitor public opinion and watch out for trouble. In addition, stations might have specific intelligence targets as, for example, in the Dhofar region where the Popular Front for the Liberation of Oman, though defeated on the battlefield, continued to infiltrate arms and propaganda from Yemen.

In all, my predecessors had done a remarkable job in building up from scratch a functioning security service. However, it lacked a cadre of capable officers rising through the Service to provide strength and future leaders. I saw remedying this as the essential task on the road to a true Omanisation. It was not enough simply to replace expatriates with Omanis if there was no capable support behind them. I came to the job with a huge advantage over my predecessors. There was a growing stream of educated school-leavers and, more importantly, in a year or two there would be university graduates from which to select, recruit, train and, most important of all, put to work under close supervision. I reported my findings and my vision of the future to the Head of the Palace Office, pointing out that, paradoxically, I had to recruit more expatriate staff to give effect to it. He was quite taken by the prospect of ISD becoming, if it was not already, the best security service in the Gulf states. He gave me a free hand.

I returned to London. Top of my list was the recruitment of a Head of Training. I had a particular officer in mind, an old Service friend, who I knew possessed the qualities for the job and who I thought might be available. He was. SIS placed in my way an officer who was moving on from the Bahrain security service. He was just the man I wanted, an experienced investigations officer to take charge of newly-trained recruits and put them through their paces. Equally serendipitously, the recently-retired MI5 Head of Technical Section was available. I engaged him to consolidate and train the technical section and lift it to the highest level of technical competence. I recruited my predecessor as Head of Training, who had by then retired from Gallagher's, to serve as Inspector of Security and, finally, I invited a female officer with whom I had worked to come out to be my PA. I wanted someone in that position without a past in the organisation.

I returned to Oman well pleased with my recruits, two of whom had fallen into my lap. Later, when the flow of graduating students began, we set up a recruitment office on the University campus and, to improve selection methods, sent an expatriate personnel officer to the UK to learn psychometric testing techniques to help identify the versatile quick-thinking young men and, yes, women we were seeking. I was to serve long enough in Oman to see the fruits of our labours as our first recruits climbed into section head positions. As time went by the expatriates all disappeared save three: The Indian doctor, the engineer responsible for air-conditioning and the investigations officer, whose continuation training role as well as his operational experience was so valued by my Omani successor that he kept him on for many more years.

As I have described, my role within the Service was a busy hands-on one. After my experience of the Libyan security service, I never had any expectation that I would soar like an eagle over an industrious ants' nest. In practice I was Controller and implementing Desk Officer combined. My outside contacts came with the job: the Commanders of the Armed Services (all British officers at the time), the Inspector-General of Police, and the Head of Palace Office who had oversight of us all. I was to work well with him over the years but always took particular care in my dealings with him (heffalump trap).

I had right of access to Sultan Qaboos. I could ask for an audience if I judged it necessary, for instance to assure myself of his approval of any operation touching a member of the royal family or to tell him something I knew that he would not like to hear. On one such occasion, I asked him at the end of the audience if my head was still on my shoulders and he sent me on my way with a wave and a laugh. I saw him many times during my long tenure of office. Solemn in public, he was vivacious in private and full of humour. In line with custom he gave me a gift at the end of the audience, a watch, a clock, a large calcite crystal, a camera in a leather case which he tried to open. I went to his side and, together, we worked out the trick and drew forth an enormous and totally impractical Nikon with every conceivable gadget.

Beyond my immediate circle of contacts lay the world of government, ministers, undersecretaries, and heads of organisations. I embarked on a course of making myself known. I began with my flight companion, the Deputy Prime Minister for Defence and Security, a largely honorific appointment, and continued with the Minister of Information then Telecommunications, Education, Commerce and so on across the whole government. Over time I developed a private liaison circle. Whenever there was information about untoward activity by ministry employees I would tell the minister privately and leave him to deal with it in his own way. The last thing ministers wanted was an officious letter from ISD or, even worse, the Palace Office.

In parallel to my official life, I expanded my private life. I took on the cook and houseboy of my predecessor and began the life of an Indian princeling. Outside stood my official car, my predecessor's blue Mercedes, which I had insisted on retaining despite pleas that I should have a new car. Alongside stood the new Nissan Desert Patrol that I had chosen. My slightest wish was a command. All I lacked was a fellow rock-climber and that too was forthcoming in the person of the British supervisor of the garden contract, himself in need of someone to climb with.

Oman is a paradise as many now know but in the simpler days before the growth of tourism it was a treasure reserved for those living there. The rugged mountains, the oases in the wadis, the forts and the watchtowers, the far stretch of the desert were ours to enjoy. The absence of rain and even the hotness of the climate added to the allure. Though development proceeded apace, we were still close enough to what it had been to sense the Arabia early travellers knew.

For me, as a rock-climber used to choosing climbs from a guide-book, Oman was uncharted territory. There was no guidebook and only a handful of known routes, some believed to have been put up by the SAS for training purposes. I thus began exploring for solid rock in the wadis near the capital area. Fixing a belay over a potential line, I top-roped down clearing the loose rock and subsequently led it with my new partner. With the idea of writing a guidebook, I made a note of each climb and assigned a name to it as tradition demands. I found this not a simple matter. I was determined to avoid dull designations such as Slab Route 2 and North Rib and usually ended up with names which had some significance for me but for no one else. One name meeting both criteria was Five O'Clock Slab, which was exactly right as it fell into shadow at that hour giving enough time for a quick climb before nightfall.

The slab in question is by the roadside just outside the capital area and I was bouldering there by myself one evening when I saw a police car pull up. Two policemen got out of the car and with the majesty of the law walked slowly across. No linguistic knowledge was needed to understand what they were about. What are you doing up there? Nothing. Get down. Clear off. As I was not asked to identify myself there was no embarrassment, but I so enjoyed the incongruity of the episode that I told the Inspector-General about it to his great amusement: the Director General of the Security Service ordered to clear off by two of his constables! He told the circle in which we moved and I never heard the end of it.

After I had been in the job for a year or so, my Omani colleagues pressed me to take up with the Palace Office their unhappiness with the perceived low status of the organisation implied by its designation as a mere department. They were also unhappy about their lack of personal status within the service and more particularly when dealing with outsiders. I agreed with them and proposed that the name of the organisation be changed from Department to Service, and that the staff be ranked in military fashion. The Palace Office agreed and the Service took the form in which it is today. Thus, ISD became ISS, Internal Security Service, and I was ranked a Liwa, the Arab equivalent of major-general. My deputy became a brigadier, the controllers colonels and so on down the line.

The Palace Office also agreed that the Service should have its own emblem. Fetching round for ideas, an Omani colleague suggested that the legendary role of the hud'hud, the hoopoe, might provide a motif. The hoopoe is mentioned in the Qur'an as one of the five birds forming part of the army of King Solomon and, relevantly, as the bearer of information to him. This was an interesting possibility. The crest of the bird is its distinguishing feature and, despite its unsavoury habits ('frequents dunghills'), I commissioned an artist who drew two versions of the bird on a shield with a scroll beneath. I took the drawings to the Sultan. He puzzled over them and with a shake of the head handed them back. No hud'hud. The emblem chosen instead was the national emblem of crossed swords and khanjar as in all the other services, as the Service expected and, as I should have foreseen, would be satisfied with none other.

However, there was still the question of the words to go on the scroll. I played around with the theme of security and safety and protection and came up with a pun of variants of the Arabic word for security: amn, amin, aman. I could tell that my Omani colleagues were not impressed but they could think of nothing better and I went ahead with it. Whether it survives to this day, I do not know. The expatriates naturally had to have a Service tie. Despite going to a maker of military ties in Bond Street this proved no easy matter and the resulting tie in some artificial fabric was so bulky when tied that I never wore it.

During my long period in office I was invited to many official occasions. I attended the lunch given occasionally by the Sultan for senior officers and officials during Eid al Fitr at the end of Ramadhan. We were called into a long narrow room on the carpet of which lay a second carpet, a yard wide and perhaps twenty feet long. On this narrow carpet the food – goat on mounds of rice, salad, dates – was laid out in repeat arrangement as if on a conveyor belt that had come to a halt. We lined up on each side of the food and the protocol attendants prowled up and down the line, rearranging guests in the correct order. The Sultan entered. We all sank to our knees and the goat was pulled apart and picked over. If you were lucky an identifiable part came your way. Supple and with short legs, I could endure the kneeling and I was practised in burying unwanted morsels in the rice.

About halfway through my time I was included in the list of those routinely invited to attend state banquets. This came about as a result of some administrative reform in which the status of service commanders was pegged with that of deputy ministers. In consequence, in addition to attending the banquets, 'His Excellency' was added to our rank to my amusement but to the embarrassment of the military commanders, whose counterparts in the Gulf states made fun of them.

The banquets, held in honour of distinguished visitors, took place in the Muscat Palace. We were entertained by the band of the Royal Guard and food was heaped onto the plate in waves of replenishment without the option of refusal. We gathered beforehand in the Palace courtyard, the ministers in their ceremonial dress, a floor-length navy-blue caftan and red and blue turban, very elegant, probably of Persian inspiration. The Court photographer, an Egyptian said to own a hotel in Cairo, darted hither and thither offering his office to those wanting to smoke. At a signal we lined up, headed by the Omanis who as usual fell into order of seniority, each knowing his place. We then filed in, followed by the Ambassadors who had assembled elsewhere. In turn, we shook hands with the guest of honour, during my time President Mitterrand, King Hussein, Vice President Bush, the Duke of Kent, the Presidents of Lebanon and Senegal and King Juan Carlos of Spain. Usually the occasion went off without hitch but there were incidents. Juan Carlos rose on hearing what he thought was the Spanish national anthem only to sit down and rise again when the band's rendering became more confident. The Lebanese President committed a breach of etiquette. There was a sharp intake of breath when, on walking out, he left the side of His Majesty to shake hands with the band.

There were the fairy tale evenings hosted by the Sultan at the palace at Seeb. After dining sumptuously al fresco, we proceeded to the Sultan's concert room to hear his orchestra of young Omanis play a selection of classical music. Chosen from all levels of society on evidence of musical ability, the boys and girls were schooled and trained from scratch and, over the years, I saw them grow to young adults. For most of the Omani guests, these after-dinner concerts were a trial unless the music was loud and fast. The Head of the Palace Office told me he got through the concert by fixing his gaze on some feature of the auditorium and gritting his teeth. He was a bagpipe man.

I regularly attended the annual Armed Forces dinner. This event took place in December in the open air at a barracks on high ground near the sea. The eight of us who were to sit at table with the Sultan stood in full view of the seated ranks of the military, talking among ourselves. My flight companion was a regular guest and so was Julian Amory, ex-minister and Tory grandee, who had a long personal association with the Sultan. In the long wait for the Sultan to appear, the feet grew cold and damp from the condensation of the sea air on the turf on which we were standing. I always wore pyjamas under my suit after the first occasion.

On assuming power the Sultan had declared tribalism and the friction and disputes that characterised Oman's history to be a thing of the past. The tribes, however, did not go away and remained a force in political and social life. The Sultan took care to achieve a tribal balance in the government and senior figures showed themselves in their tribal areas. The Head of the Palace Office invited me to visit him in his fiefdom. A camel was slaughtered and I was force-fed to repletion on camel kebabs before being taken to dine elsewhere on goat and rice. The Minister of Agriculture invited me to his fiefdom in the Interior to inspect an experimental plot. Afterwards, we sat on a carpet on the hillside under the waning sun looking out across the desert, eating dates and little lamb kebabs cooked a short distance away. These senior figures were always accompanied by a silent retinue of fellow tribesmen, guards, drivers, and servants.

I was the guest of the British Ambassador on many occasions. He invited me to dinners for visiting ministers and, as part of the programme, closetted me with them for a chat. I attended a dinner party for Prince Philip who was in Oman on World Wildlife Fund affairs. He was rather distant during drinks (who can blame him) and he would not have derived much pleasure from the dinner arrangement. We were arranged in tables of four and, at his table, the Duke faced the Personal Representative of the Sultan, an elderly and taciturn relative with little English, and on his left and right, preening themselves, the European wives of members of the Omani royal family. I attended a reception on board the Royal Yacht when it called at Muscat during the honeymoon voyage of Prince Charles and Diana. The Ambassador introduced me to Prince Charles. On being told my role, he said, fiddling with his cuffs, 'That must be very interesting,' to which all I could say was 'yes' before being plucked aside to make way for the next in line.

On occasion the Sultan's Personal Representative took Eid greetings on the Sultan's behalf. We gathered outside, some fifty of us, for the usual long wait, some seated, some standing. The Minister of Defence beckoned me to an empty seat at his side, on the other side of which sat the Grand Mufti, a small unassuming man in the short dishdasha worn by the pious. I had not met him. He shook my hand and began to tell me something in a tone of self-exculpation. I could not follow and the Minister explained, 'he says he only sat down because he has a bad back'. And that was the sum total of my dealings with the senior religious cleric of Oman.

Eventually, the doors opened. Inside there were two long rows of chairs facing each other and, between them at the far end of the room, the Personal Representative was seated on a throne-like chair. We filed up to him, nodded and murmured the appropriate words, then turned and took a seat. When all were seated, servants carrying billowing incense burners fumigated us, stopping so that each could waft the smoke under the armpits and into the beard. Then followed the halwa, a thick, sweet, and very sticky goo. It was presented in a tub like a baby's bath carried by two bearers and into it you plunged the first two fingers of the right hand and scooped a glob into your mouth. You then sat, sticky fingers raised, waiting for the man with ewer, bowl, and towel to catch up. When all had done, thin reedy coffee was poured by servants juggling five or six cups who moved back and forth along the line. Next to come was the rose water and spirits rose when the dispensers were brought in. An Arab proverb says, 'After the rosewater there is no staying,' but not yet: the host, who had sat silent and motionless throughout the proceedings, had still to rise and, when he did, there was a rush for the door.

I was frustrated by my inability to get a grip on Arabic off the page. I was assiduous in my studies and determined to learn this fascinating language. At 6.30 each morning, bed tea was brought and I opened my book. I have always learned principally from the book because, in my deafness, consonants are confused and Arabic has groups of them which are very similar but sound the same to me. Furthermore, learning a language in later years is a battle with reduced memory retention. Notwithstanding, I learned enough to be able to check the translation of my letters and occasionally spot a grammatical error. I gave speeches in Arabic, a long address on the occasion of the distribution of the medal to commemorate the twentieth anniversary of the Sultan's accession, and short speeches whenever I presented long service medals. Despite this body of knowledge, my conversation did not progress beyond simple exchanges and I quickly got lost at meetings, drowning in a sea of sounds, clutching at passing words.

My work took me to every part of the country and wherever I went I looked out for rock-climbing possibilities. These were usually passing fantasies as I did not have the time or confidence to lay siege to the big rock walls I saw. In my search for smaller cliffs close to home, I found a narrow wadi flanked by cliffs rising to some 350 ft which were in the shade by mid-afternoon. Perfect. Like the pioneer climbers of the 1920s I climbed anything that I could get up, mostly in the Severe/Very Severe grade but some harder, including one later rated E2. Between 1985 and 1992, I put up fifty-eight first ascents of which twenty-eight were in this wadi, almost all of them with the garden manager as second. My long-standing UK climbing partner, Harry Woodbridge, came out every year and, with the arrival on the scene of Gilles Rappeneau, the representative of the French oil company ELF, the level of climbing went up a grade with the bolted routes he developed.

In 1988 I received a letter from Tony Howard of Troll Wall and Wadi Rum fame, in which he proposed carrying out an adventure tourism survey in Oman as a development project as he had done in Jordan. It would be a labour of love and self-funded. I took the proposal to the Minister of Commerce, under whom tourism came, and persuaded him to contribute 20,000 rials in support. Howard brought a large party, all climbers, with him: his partner, two French guides, an Italian photographer, a leading female climber from Switzerland and a British cave expert.

The party spent the whole of 1989 in the field. They ranged over the 200-mile long mountain chain on the eastern seaboard and explored Mussandam in the north and Dhofar in the south. The outcome was a detailed report of 202 pages with interleaved photographs and suggestions for follow-up action. However, it came too early in the development of tourism in Oman, to which there was resistance in remoter areas, and the report was shelved. The only action taken was that by the Director of Tourism who opened a tourism agency.

At times I climbed with the party and memorably went with Tony Howard to open a route on Jebel Misht, Mount Cockscomb, well named as the mountain culminates in a curtain of cliffs reaching 1,500 ft at their highest. With great confidence he led the climb on sight in a single day as planned. For me it was the climb of a lifetime and is listed with our names in the guidebook: 23/12 1988 South East Pillar VI-350m. Having left boots behind to save weight, the walk-off after the climb in our climbing shoes was long and painful.

We had barely met up with Howard's partner and my PA who had driven round the mountain to meet us when we were approached by an Omani who appeared, seemingly out of nowhere, in this remote place, curious to know what we were up to. Soon all was explained as the Omani, an Army captain, spoke good English. He insisted that we accompany him to his father's house, hospitality we could not refuse, so we followed him further into the back of beyond. We were welcomed by the family and, installed in the majlis, struggled to keep awake, waiting for the coffee.

Some weeks later, the Captain came unannounced to the office. After greetings we talked for a while during which time, as custom demanded, no mention was made of the purpose of his visit. To precipitate this I half rose then sat down as the Captain hastened to explain that he had come on behalf of his brother, unbeknown to me, a clerk in Registry. His brother had taken advantage of the willingness of the Government in the early years to fund university training for anyone willing to undergo it and he had been accepted by a Saudi university for medical training. His brother failed his first year and failed again at the end of the second and third year and yet again in the fourth year, which he had been warned was his last chance. He had returned to his place of work in Registry which, the Captain observed, did not make use of the medical knowledge he possessed despite his failures. Could he not work in the clinic? I said 'Allah karim,' which was the standard reply to such a request, implying 'I'll see but can't promise'. I related this sorry tale to my Omani deputy. Without a pause for thought he said 'no way'.

After seven and a half years 'on scat' I was Omanised, the last of the British service chiefs to make way. I asked the Sultan if I could stay on for a while and was appointed Advisor to the Head of the Palace Office. I was congratulated on my new appointment but I was under no illusion: it was a parking place. When I asked the Head of the Palace Office about the hours the office kept, he replied, 'Come when you like. Don't come at all.' I did however write two papers for him, one of which was about how to tackle high-level corruption, but at that time no one had the courage or the folly to take action.

I used the extra six months to write Rock Climbing in Oman. I needed to revisit cliffs to draw diagrams of the lines followed by routes, take photographs and check descriptions, to transcribe my notes and raise money to pay for publication. Though recognising that all climbing guides are out of date by the time they are published I nonetheless stated in the Introduction that, despite the profusion of rock, Oman would not become a mecca for rock climbers because of the heat, absence of water, difficulty of access and the unreliable nature of the rock. How wrong I was. Alpine guides with time on their hands in the winter came and opened routes on the huge walls. Twenty years after my guide, a new guide was published, crammed with routes including a few of mine. My book is now of antiquarian interest while the cliffs of 'my' wadi have been separated by a high-speed road leading to the hotel on the beach at its end.

I left Oman on the 1st of April 1993, eight years to the day after my arrival. Some years earlier I had been awarded the Order of Oman and, at my final audience, the Sultan presented me with a ceremonial khanjar 'to hang above the mantelpiece,' and instructed that my name be added to the list of Private Guests invited each year to Oman for the National Day celebrations. So I left Oman with the reassurance of return. It was not goodbye but au revoir.

Chamonix

On leaving Oman I was accompanied by Sue Pickthall whom I had brought out to be my PA or, as she was more grandly known by the Omanis, Director of the DG's Office. I had come to know Sue when she was posted to the Training Department when I was in the chair. A graduate from Edinburgh University with Spanish and Portuguese, she was snapped up by SIS and after service as station secretary in Rio and Buenos Aires she was bridged to officer status. Finding each other like-minded, we started an association which took a decisive step forward after her promising performance on a steep, damp limestone cliff.

Sue shared my private life in Oman. Together we explored Oman, climbed, drove across the Wahiba sands, visited the oryx sanctuary and sailed on the Service dhow. I did not know we had a dhow until Admin requested permission to sell it as nobody used it. It was a fine vessel. Small and motor-powered, it was nevertheless the real thing so I had it given a lick of varnish and it became the DG's dhow. Our usual destination was a bay accessible only by sea which we had to ourselves. Today it is a beach resort 'a short drive from Muscat'.

We took our holidays together. We would fly to Frankfurt, hire a car and head for the mountains. We walked the Austrian alps in the summer and skied in them in the winter. We were by that time reasonably proficient skiers. We had started with lessons at a dry-ski slope outside London in Training Department days. I was then in my early fifties and, with children gone their various ways and my bank balance at last in the black, I had the time and money to take up skiing. Like all climbers I made the unjustified assumption that skiing would come naturally. Of course it did not, and we worked our way up to competence in a succession of Ski Club of Great Britain holidays.

During our time in Oman we went on one of these holidays to Aspen, Colorado. I mentioned it to our CIA colleague and was surprised days later to be invited to visit Washington on the way, all expenses paid. We flew by Concorde and, after three days' work and play in Washington, flew on to Denver where we were taken to see the bison grazing before grazing on them at lunch. We were then put in a stretch limousine and driven the 160 miles to Aspen. What style!

About halfway through our time in Oman we had our winter ski holiday at Megève, on the flank of Mont Blanc. We were rather taken with the resort and toyed with the idea of buying an apartment there as a holiday base. I mentioned this to Gilles Rappeneau. He was aghast. Ah, non! A quoi penses-tu, Alec? Megève? The skiing was mediocre and it had no summer climbing. Chamonix, where he had a small chalet, was the only place to be. When we visited him the following summer, he had an apartment lined up for us to see. There was no escape: we bought the apartment in Argentière at the head of the Chamonix valley, a few minutes' walk from the lifts.

It was to this apartment rather than to Sue's house in London we headed on leaving Oman. We had spent many holidays there and our plan was to see if we wished to make it our main home. So began our athletic retirement life; I was sixty-three and Sue was forty-seven and rarely a day passed when we did not ski or climb. When the lifts closed we headed for London and, when they re-opened, back to Chamonix, thus spending the autumn and spring in London. Life was good, and after a year or so we began to look around for a chalet to give us a garden and more room. We were very choosy and it was a year before we found what we were looking for and moved to a chalet on the edge of Chamonix with, as the advertisement said, 'une vue imprenable sur Mont Blanc', an unbeatable view of the tumbling glaciers of the highest mountain in Europe. We lived there for twenty years.

We took our skiing very seriously and by dint of unremitting practice achieved a level which emboldened us to look higher to ski touring, hut-to-hut ski mountaineering. We booked an introductory course and learned to do the excruciating uphill kick-turn, wobbling on one unstable foot. Thereafter we went on many high excursions in Austria, France, Italy, and Switzerland, including the celebrated High Route from Chamonix to Zermatt.

Our guide on one of these trips, Yvon Estienne, turned out to be one of the two French guides who had put up the famous French Route on Jebel Misht in 1979. He told me that the ascent was filmed by a team from the Ministry of Information and, when I was next in Oman, I asked the Minister for a copy if the film could be found in the archives. It was forthcoming and I gave it to Estienne, delighted to see himself as the young man wearing the clocked stockings and breeches of yesteryear.

We took up ski de fond or langlauf. There seems to be no English name for this form of skiing on narrow whippy plastic skis which is deceptively simple but has more to it than meets the eye. With increasing proficiency, we sought out long and challenging circuits and our culminating achievement was an unguided four day hut-to-hut traverse of the Jura mountain ridge, much of it on untracked snow.

I also enjoyed the skating form of ski de fond, exhilarating but hard on ageing lungs going uphill. When I thought I was good enough I took part in a local marathon. I completed the course, finishing last as I expected but by a discouragingly large margin. Then well into my seventies, I accepted that I was not up to the physical demand of the race with its long ascents and dropped down to the twelve kilometre race in succeeding years, in which I managed to keep within my target time of one hour, by no means the last to finish.

The lifts opened in mid-June but climbing at higher altitudes did not commonly begin until the snow had retreated, opening up straightforward access to the cliffs. At lower level there was no shortage of cliffs on which to get into shape and Sue and I climbed several days a week. On leave from Oman, Rappeneau introduced me to harder routes on high cliffs. I climbed also with his friends, with local British climbers and with Harry Woodbridge who came out for a month each year. Sue was glad enough to see me go off with them and be spared the ordeal but she climbed uncomplainingly, leading the occasional Grade 4 pitch and, once, one of Grade 5. However it was not all rock-climbing. We raised our eyes from the rock in front of our noses and enjoyed the mountains for themselves. Together we walked the glaciers and high snowfields and climbed Mont Blanc.

We had many visitors, summer and winter, regularly from the extended family but also from skiing and climbing friends formed over the years and colleagues from the Service and Oman, including two Omanis with their families who in their robes cut a figure in town. I skied with my grandchildren during their formative years and took my brother, one year younger, climbing despite his shaky Parkinson's hands. My son came to Chamonix for an extended stay between jobs and liked to go off on his own to camp overnight with marmots for company.

We had local French friends formed through the Chamonix bridge club. The hills were alive with sound of cards being shuffled. There were four other clubs within easy reach and it was possible to play at one or the other every day of the week. As a summer as well as a winter resort, Chamonix has a range of visitors other than climbers and skiers and bridge was one of the activities supported by the municipality. The weekly tournaments were open to all and were a far livelier scene than the usual sedate proceedings with arguments, recriminations and threats to walk out in a variety of languages.

It was at bridge that the dark cloud first appeared. I noticed Sue in difficulty and that her standard of play had dropped. I wanted to believe that this was due to her eyesight but two expensive pairs of glasses later, the optician took me aside to say that Sue should see a consultant ophthalmologist. When next in London we did so, and at the conclusion of his examination the specialist said that the next step was to see a neurologist. With foreboding, that was arranged and, after tests and scans, the verdict was that Sue was suffering from Early Onset Alzheimer's, life expectancy ten to twelve years. Coming on top of the type one diabetes which had been identified two years earlier this was a cruel blow, but Sue took it in her stride with her usual fortitude. 'We just have to get on with it,' she would say, and throughout the years of decline never showed any sign of self-pity. Twelve years, however, was a long way off. Life continued.

I went every year to Oman for the National Day celebrations as a member of the party of Private Guests invited by the Sultan. Numbering thirty or so, it was composed of politicians, the Chief of Defence Staff, ex-Chiefs of SIS and prominent figures in the world of business plus the dozen or so of us who had borne the heat of the day, including the diminishing few whose association with Sultan dated back to his early days in office. When Sue and I married in 1995, she became eligible to join the party for those five days of privilege and spectacle which concluded with dinner at the Palace with concert, of course, to follow.

A letter came one day from the CIA head of station in Oman during my final years saying that he would be travelling to the Middle East with the Operational Director of the CIA, who hoped we might meet during their stop-over in Geneva. This man, who had risen to be the CIA equivalent of the SIS Chief, had been my opposite number in Benghazi. On the appointed day, Sue and I drove to a restaurant on the shore of Lake Geneva and there we sat with my old friend and colleague of thirty years earlier. In the course of the meal, he presented me with the US Medal for Outstanding Service. On the back of the medal my name is inscribed with the words 'In recognition of eight years of superior co-operation and assistance 1985 – 1993'.

On the eve of my eighty-fourth birthday I went with Harry on the last day of his visit for a farewell climb on the nearby roadside cliff. It was a hot muggy afternoon and the cliff was crowded. The only climb available was a discontinuous 4+ route that I had already climbed two or three times. At the first testing move I failed to apply enough pull to a side-pressure hold and my foot slipped off. Oops! I said to myself then bang, oblivion. It was painless. I had been ten feet above the last bolt and fell to a ledge more than ten feet below it. I was expertly brought to the ground by guides and prodded into life. I had lost my hearing aid. At the hospital, X-rays revealed that I had a broken pelvis and fractured skull. I was lucky to be alive, and lucky also to get my hearing aid back which had been spotted on the ground.

By pure chance, a local British climbing friend arrived on the scene just after the accident and took charge. He notified my younger daughter and his wife looked after Sue, who could no longer self-administer her insulin, until my daughter arrived the next day, followed by her sister a day or two later. My stay in hospital, at first expected to be four days, extended to twelve when a bleed on the brain developed. The meals were something to look forward to as the French demand to be well fed in hospital but the tempting dishes on offer proved disappointingly bland. It took a surprisingly long time to realise that I had lost my sense of smell and with it most of my sense of taste.

It so happened that we had sold the chalet before the accident, having taken the decision that we had to return to London because of Sue's decline. Strictly forbidden to do anything, I watched on helplessly as my daughter ruthlessly disposed of the accumulation of possessions that had built up in our twenty-five years in the valley. My skiing grandchildren came out to say goodbye to the chalet and Sue's cousin and husband drove out and took back with them what had been saved for London. On the day of our departure climbing friends gathered to see us off. We waved goodbye to them and to Chamonix and turned to face London without enthusiasm.

Some months after the accident, I began to climb regularly at the Westway climbing wall in London. For my eight-fifth birthday Sue's cousin gave me a present of two days' climbing in North Wales with a guide. We climbed a few old favourites but my performance told me that my outdoor climbing days were numbered. Meanwhile Sue's condition steadily worsened and the time came, after two years in London, to move to more manageable accommodation close to my elder daughter in Herefordshire. I then transferred my gymnastics to the climbing wall in Gloucester and with friends made there I climbed on local cliffs a few more times, the last at the age of eighty-seven. Within feet of leaving the ground I knew I was climbing my last climb. I no longer had the sustained physical attack required. However I did not abandon the climbing wall and continued to struggle up it, if only for the satisfaction of still being able to do it.

All the while, Sue retreated further and further into her own lost world. When I could no longer care for her she went into a nursing home in the summer of 2018 and, on the 24th of January 2019, she bowed to the inevitable, ten years after her diagnosis, aged seventy-one.

Epilogue

Like the Mock Turtle, I sit on the shore of life contemplating the days when I was a real turtle, and what days they were, as adventure followed adventure. Fortune led my steps to the door of SIS and I was admitted, pinching myself in disbelief, alarmed and exhilarated by its imagined demands. The time would come when I in my turn, as Chairman of the Final Selection Board, admitted nervous postulants to our calling, as some colleagues did indeed regard it. For me, the Service was the last refuge of the romantic.

When I joined I was a mixture of over-confidence and under-confidence, a parvenu. I had no sense of entitlement and looked out on the world through the window of the council house and never lost sight of those who came behind. As I advanced in the Service I did not feel enlarged by increased authority, or indeed find any need to exert it as those in my charge did what was required of them without demur. With each step up, I counted on this voluntary compliance, never more so than on taking over in Oman. When I issued my first order, about dress to be worn in the office, I held my breath.

Revisiting my life has brought home to me the scale of the debt I owe to my parents for their unhesitating support. Back to Bexleyheath was a feature of our life and we could not have managed without it.

To my old Service I owe the career I enjoyed and the gift of Oman. We were a band of brothers with diverse talents and languages held together by a remarkable esprit de corps. Whenever we get together we reminisce till the small hours and on parting, as we stretch and yawn, we always say how lucky we have been.

Who should have such fortune!

Matador

For exclusive discounts on Matador titles,
sign up to our occasional newsletter at
troubador.co.uk/bookshop